IS THE CHURCH TOO ASIAN?
REFLECTIONS ON THE
ECUMENICAL COUNCILS

NORMAN TANNER

Is the Church Too Asian?
Reflections on the Ecumenical Councils

Norman Tanner

Chavara Institute of Indian and Inter-religious Studies
Rome
&
Dharmaram Publications
Bangalore

2002

Is the Church Too Asian?
Reflections on the Ecumenical Councils

by
Norman Tanner

Placid Lectures 2001
Organized by CIIS, Rome

© CIIS, Rome

Published by: Chavara Institute of Indian and Inter-religious
   Studies,
   Corso Vittorio Emanuele-294/10
   00186, Rome, Italy
   &
   Dharmaram Publications
   Dharmaram College P.O.
   Dharmaram College,
   Bangalore- 560 029, India

Typeset and Cover Design: Jinu George

Printed at: National Printing Press, Koramangala, Bangalore

Price: Hardbound: Rs. 75.00; US$7
   Paperback : Rs. 60.00; US$5

ISBN: 81-86861-48-3

Contents

Preface 7
Abbreviations 9
Introduction 11

Chapter 1: The Early Church 13
    Places 14
    Participants 15
    Greek Philosophy? 17
    Creeds and Teachings of the Councils 18
        Nicaea I 19
        Constantinople I 20
        Ephesus 22
        Chalcedon 25
        Constantinople II and III 27
        Nicaea II 28
    Western Influence in a Minor Key 29
    Mentality of the Decrees 30

Chapter 2: Middle Ages and Trent 33
    Status of the Councils 33
    Little Development in Doctrines 39
    Inferiority Complex of the West 44
    Decrees on Church Order 47
    Council of Trent 50

Chapter 3: Vatican I and II 55
    Vatican I 55
    Vatican II 59

Preparation 60
First Session, Autumn 1962 63
The Progressive Majority 69
Third Session, Autumn 1964 70
The Church in the Modern World 70
Priests 80
Marriage 81
Conclusion 82

Conclusion and the Future 85

Index 87

Preface

The text of this booklet is a revised version of the **Placid Lectures** given – under the same title – at Chavara Institute of Indian and Interreligious Studies (CIIS) in Rome in December 2001. I am grateful to Professor Thomas Aykara CMI, Director of the Institute, for the honour of inviting me to give the lectures. I thank him, Fr. Justine Koyipuram, Procurator-General of the Congregation of Mary Immaculate (CMI), and other members of the Congregation, as well as all those who attended the lectures, for their warm welcome and hospitality and for their many helpful comments and questions during the discussion time that followed each lecture.

Abbreviations

Alberigo, *Vatican II* G. Alberigo (ed.), *History of Vatican II*, 3 of 5 vols. so far (Maryknoll and Leuven, 1995-). Page references for vols. 4 and 5 are to the Italian version, *Storia del concilio Vaticano II*, 5 vols. (Bologna and Leuven, 1995-2001), abbreviated to: Alberigo, *Vaticano II*.

Decrees *Decrees of the Ecumenical Councils*, N. Tanner (ed.), 2 vols. (London and Georgetown, 1990)

DTC *Dictionnaire de Théologie Catholique* (Paris, 1903-50)

EEC *Encyclopedia of the Early Church*, A. Di Berardino (ed.), 2 vols. (Cambridge: James Clarke, 1992)

Grillmeier, *Christ* A. Grillmeier, *Christ in Christian Tradition*, 2 vols. so far (London: Mowbrays, 1975-)

Jedin, *History* H. Jedin (ed.), *History of the Church*, 10 vols. (London: Burns & Oates, 1980)

Kelly, *Creeds* J.N.D. Kelly, *Early Christian Creeds*, 3rd edn. (London: Longman, 1972)

ODB *The Oxford Dictionary of Byzantium*, ed. A.P. Kazhdan, 3 vols. (New York and Oxford, 1991).

Tanner, *Councils*   N. Tanner, *The Councils of the Church: A Short History* (New York: Crossroad, 2001)

Introduction

The claim, 'The Church is too Western', has been familiar to us for some time. Indeed, the terrible events in New York and Washington last September 2001, and some of the responses to them, have heightened for many the perceived dichotomy between East and West. A largely non-christian Asia, it is argued, has been struggling, at times violently, against the dominance and arrogance of the christian West. On the one hand we are aware of Christianity's roots in Asia. Christ and his disciples were Asians, the early Church was predominantly Asian. On the other hand, so the argument goes, the Church was quickly taken over by western ways of thought – notably Greek philosophy – and by westerners. The centre of the Church moved to Rome and the West and remained there.

Dialogue between East and West, between Christianity and the other world religions of Asia, are high priorities of our time. Fr Placid Podipara CMI, in whose honour this lecture series is named, was well known for his promotion of dialogue and understanding between the religions of Asia and the West and for his initiatives in recovering the genuinely Indian features of Christianity, especially with respect to the liturgy of the Syro-Malabar rite. These lectures seek to follow in his footsteps, in a small way, by examining one dimension of Asia's contribution to Christianity and thereby questioning the assumption of western dominance over the Church. The aspect chosen, as the sub-title of the lectures indicates, is the tradition of the twenty-one ecumenical and general councils of the Church from Nicaea I in 325 to Vatican II in 1962-5. These great assemblies form a hugely influential chain in the history of the Church, of the undivided Church of East and West in the first millennium, and of the western church in the second millennium. How great was the Asian contribution to them?

Chapter 1: The Early Church

In this first lecture I wish to look at the ecumenical councils of the first millennium of Christianity, those that are often called the seven councils of the undivided Church: before, that is, the beginning of the sad schism between the churches of East and West in the eleventh century. They are the councils of Nicaea I in 325, Constantinople I in 381, Ephesus in 431, Chalcedon in 451, Constantinople II in 553, Constantinople III in 680-1, and Nicaea II in 787.[1] The Asian contribution to them was great. Indeed we may say it – or at least the eastern contribution – was dominant.

---

[1] Two councils whose ecumenical status is disputed will be left out of consideration, Trullo in 692 and Constantinople IV in 869-70. The council of Trullo, or 'in Trullo' (called thus because it was held in the domed hall – Greek, *en tō Troullo* of the emperor's palace in Constantinople), which promulgated 102 decrees of a mostly disciplinary nature, forming the basis of the canon law of the eastern Church, is regarded as ecumenical in the East. (Though usually it is seen as the completion of the fifth and sixth ecumenical councils of Constantinople II and III – which issued no disciplinary canons – and hence its other name of 'Quinisext', rather than as a separate council.) Its status in the West has been disputed but since the early Middle Ages it has usually been omitted from the list of ecumenical councils. On the other hand, the fourth council of Constantinople in 870-1, whose principal business was the deposition of patriarch Photius of Constantinople, has for long been included among the ecumenical councils in the West but is not regarded as ecumenical by the eastern Church. In recent years the ecumenicity of both councils has been reexamined especially by western scholars, for the most part leading to an acceptance of the arguments of the eastern Church in both cases. For a brief discussion of the issues see, Tanner, *Councils*, pp. 41-3. For Trullo, see especially, G. Nedungatt and M. Featherstone (eds.), *The Council of Trullo Revisited*, Kanonika, 6 (Rome, 1995).

Places

The first and most obvious point is that four of the seven councils were held in Asia: Nicaea I and II, Ephesus and Chalcedon. The other three were held in Constantinople and therefore just in Europe, if one accepts the Bosphorus as the boundary between Asia and Europe.

Here a short diversion regarding the definition of Asia is in order. I am no geographer but we know that Asia has been understood differently in the course of history, or perhaps rather there has been a development of meaning. The word is ancient but its origin is unclear. *Enclycopedia Britannica* says, 'The Greeks used it to designate the lands situated to the East of their homeland. It is also believed that the name may be derived from the Assyrian *asu* meaning "east". Another possible explanation is that it was originally a local name given to the plains of Ephesus and gradually extended to include Anatolia (contemporary Asia Minor) ... and the rest of the continent.'[2] Hecataeus, the Greek geographer, in his map around 500 BCE, divided the world into Europe and Asia (which included Africa). The province of Asia in the Roman Empire stretched, at its greatest extent, from the Aegean coast in the West to a point beyond Philomelium (modern Aksehir) in the east. It was only much later, as a result of European voyages from the fifteenth century onwards, that the continent of Asia came to have its modern definition.

Throughout the period of the seven councils in question, from 325 to 787, the distinction between the mainly Greek and Syriac speaking East and the Latin speaking West was more significant, at least in the eyes of those living within the Roman

---

[2] *The New Encyclopaedia Britannica* (15th edition, printing of 1992), vol. 14 (Macropedia), p. 128 (Asia).

Empire, than that between Asia and Europe. That Constantinople, the site of three of the councils, was in the East, indeed was the capital of the eastern empire, and lay close to if not within what was then considered to be Asia, is, therefore, more relevant to our thesis than that today it lies, renamed as Istanbul, just within the more recent definition of Europe's boundaries.

Participants

Another striking point is that the overwhelming majority of participants at all seven councils came from the East and most were Asians. At the first council, Nicaea I in 325, there were two legates of the bishop of Rome and at most half a dozen bishops from the western church. All the other bishops whose sees are known – some 220 of the total participation of probably 250-300 bishops – were from the eastern church, the largest group coming from within the borders of modern Turkey.[3] At Constantinople I in 381 there were no representatives of the western church, all 150 or so bishops who attended came from dioceses in the East.[4] In effect it was a council of the eastern church and was promoted to ecumenical status when its creed was endorsed by the council of Chalcedon in 451. At the other five ecumenical councils, papal legates attended but there were very few other representatives of the western church: the large majority of bishops came from the East and most from present-day Asia.[5]

---

[3]I. Ortiz de Urbina, *Nicée et Constantinople*, Histoire des conciles oecuméniques, ed. G. Dumeige, vol. 1 (Paris, 1963), pp. 300-1 (map); E. Honigmann, 'The original lists of the members of the council of Nicaea, the Robber Synod and the Council of Chalcedon,' *Byzantion*, 16 (1942-3), p. 22; *DTC*, xi, cols. 402-3.

[4]Ortiz de Urbina, *Nicée et Constantinople*, op. cit., p. 170; *DTC*, iii, col. 1228.

[5]*DTC*, ii, col. 2192, iii, cols. 1236, 1266, v, cols. 142-3, xi, cols. 419-20;

All seven councils, moreover, were summoned, presided over, either directly or through their officials, and their decrees promulgated, by the eastern emperor of the day and, in two cases, also by the empress. All of them were Europeans yet the fact that they belonged to the Greek-speaking East, either by birth and upbringing or by adoption, is perhaps more significant. Constantine I, emperor at the time of Nicaea I, was probably born at Niš (then *Naisos*) in modern Serbia. As a commander in the emperor Galerius's army he had travelled as far East as Persia and as emperor he moved the centre of power eastwards, towards Asia, by establishing a second capital at Constantinople, the city he named after himself. Theodosius I, a Spaniard, was the eastern emperor at the time of the first council of Constantinople in 381. Theodosius II, the emperor who tried to control the stormy council of Ephesus, was a citizen of Constantinople *par excellence*. Born and brought up in the city, he lived there most of the time during his long years as emperor. By then the western empire was in collapse and his reign illustrates well the extent to which the centre of power now lay in the East. His sister, the empress Pulcheria, who was the key organiser of the council of Chalcedon in 451, even more so than her husband, the emperor Marcion, was also born and brought up in Constantinople and the city was her power-base, though in many ways she was pro-western. Justinian I, who managed the ill-fated third council of Constantinople II in 553, was born at Bederiana in the Balkans and he too based himself at Constantinople during his long reign as emperor. It was likewise the capital city for emperor Constantine IV and empress Irene, who presided over the last two councils in question, Constantinople III in 680-1 and Nicaea II in 787.[6]

Honigmann, 'Original Lists', op. cit., p. 62

[6]Biographical details of these emperors and empresses may conveniently be found in their entries in *EEC* and *ODB*.

In short, the complaint of Christians in the West, regarding the location, composition and organisation of the first seven councils, might well have been, 'The Church is too Asian, or at least too eastern'. Just the reverse of the talk today! I have not found any contemporary quotations to this effect – I would be very pleased to learn of any -- but it would be surprising if this sense of imbalance did not exist. Maybe westerners were more than usually patient and understanding. After all, they could see the western empire had collapsed and was incapable of staging a council of the whole church even if it wanted to, whereas the eastern empire had survived and it alone had the capacity to host an ecumenical council.

Greek Philosophy?

But what of the argument that the ecumenical councils of the early Church were dominated by western thought and concepts, principally Greek philosophy? Before we look in detail at the creeds and other doctrinal statements issued by these councils, we should ask the preliminary question of whether Greek philosophy was basically western and European or, rather, more eastern and Asian. The West has, perhaps, hijacked Greek philosophy – above all the philosophy of Plato and Aristotle – into its own chariot and the surprise is that Asia and the East has not protested more. Asia has so many cultural and intellectual roots that it perhaps feels less need to be possessive about its Greek roots. Europe, on the other hand, especially western Europe, without the richness of Asia's origins, has been desperate to find its intellectual roots and especially since the nineteenth century secular elements, which dislike much emphasis upon Europe's christian inspiration, have discovered these roots in classical Greek thought. The point was brought home to me starkly by the very differing entrances of Greece and my own country, Britain, to the European Economic Community (now called the European Union), if I may be allowed a personal reflection here. Whereas Britain had to struggle for many years to be admitted to this Community, including suffering two vetoes to its membership in the 1960s, Greece was offered membership almost straightaway after applying. The argument, occasionally stated openly but more usually implicit, was that Greece must be admitted since it is the birthplace of European thought: a European Community or Union without Greece was unthinkable.

However, when we examine this thesis of the western orientation of Greek thought and civilization more closely, much of it disintegrates. The most obvious point is that its language was Greek, the most widespread *lingua franca* of the eastern empire including the Asian parts of it, whereas that of the western empire was Latin. The Greek world looked eastwards much more than westwards. It was in contact with the thought of Persia and further East, uninterested in the illiterate peoples of western Europe. Alexander the Great campaigned eastwards as far as the Indus valley, and south into Africa, not towards Italy or France. Athens was much closer to Aleppo and perhaps to the civilizations of the Indus valley and beyond than to Paris or London. M.L. West, Walter Burkert and other scholars have revealed much about this eastern face of Hellenism in recent years.[7] It merits further research.

Creeds and Teachings of the Councils

It comes as no surprise, therefore, that a pronounced eastern face appears in the creeds and other statements of the

---

[7]M.L. West, *Early Greek Philosophy and the Orient* (Clarendon Press, Oxford, 1971); idem, *The East Face of Helicon: West Asiatic Elements in Greek Poetry and Myth* (Clarendon Press, Oxford, 1997); W. Burkert, *The Orientalizing Revolution: Near Eastern Influence on Greek Culture in the Early Archaic Age* (Harvard University Press, 1992). See also E.R. Dodds, *The Greeks and the Irrational* (University of California Press, 1959).

seven councils in question. In the first place and very importantly, the language of all of them – both of their proceedings and of the decrees they issued – was Greek, the language of the eastern empire.

Nicaea I

Regarding the first council of Nicaea in 325, the origin of its creed -- the first version of the Nicene creed – is debated. However, it was surely eastern rather than western. Somewhere in Syria or Palestine, perhaps Jerusalem, is now thought to be the most likely place, rather than Caesarea in modern Turkey, the see of Eusebius of Caesarea, which used to be preferred. The creed of a local church was evidently taken over by the council of Nicaea as the core of its creed and various anti-Arian clauses were added to it.[8] The thesis that the western bishop, Ossius of Cordoba, was largely responsible for the inclusion of the crucial word 'homoousios'(ὁμοούσιος) – asserting the consubstantiality of the Son with the Father – finds few supporters now. There was probably some western influence upon the choice of the word. Tertullian, for example, had spoken of *unius substantiae* (though not, so far as we know, of *consubstantialis*) and Ossius may well have played a part. But the word was already in use in the east, in both theology and philosophy. Indeed, the main difficulty with it seems to have originated in Asia, namely that the word, when used to describe the relationship between Father and Son, had been condemned by the council of Antioch in 268, in the Paul of Samosata affair, so that Nicaea had to justify itself by arguing that it was using the word in a spiritual sense of consubstantiality, rather than the material sense that, allegedly, the council of Antioch had in mind in its condemnation. Both a western and, more

---

[8]Kelly, *Creeds*, pp. 205-30.

prominently, an eastern ancestry leading to the choice of 'homoousios' seems the most likely hypothesis.[9]

The context of Nicaea's twenty disciplinary canons – the second major contribution of the council – also seems to be predominantly Asian. Most obviously, they were promulgated by a council held in Asia. As for their sources, the absence of any surviving *acta* (minutes of the meetings of the council and other contemporary background material) makes it difficult to speak with certainty but a number of the canons appear to have been based on those of earlier local councils in Asia Minor, notably the councils of Ancyra (modern Ankara) in 314 and Neocaesarea in 315/324.[10] The legislation was intended primarily for the churches of the East but it became the first code – the template – of canon law for the universal Church. It covered a wide range of issues concerning both laity and clergy: conditions for ordination, morals and status of clergy; hierarchy among bishops; baptism and eucharist; reconciliation through various forms of penance; holding of regular local councils; deaconesses; posture in prayer.[11] All this was given to the universal Church by Asia rather than the West.

Constantinople I

The second ecumenical council of the Church, Constantinople I in 381, is known chiefly for the revised version of the Nicene creed which has remained until today the principal

---

[9] Kelly, *Creeds*, pp. 242-54; R.P.C. Hanson, *The Search for the Christian Doctrine of God: The Arian Controversy 318-381* (Edinburgh, 1988), pp.190-202; Ortiz de Urbina, *Nicée et Constantinople,* op. cit., pp. 82-7.

[10] Ortiz de Urbina, *Nicée et Constantinople*, op. cit., p. 95; *Decrees*, i, notes on pp. 6-16.

[11] *Decrees*, i, pp. 6-16. The canons entered the western church principally through Dionysius Exiguus's translation of them into Latin in the early sixth century.

creed of all the mainline christian churches. Here, too, the Asian influence is preeminent. First, because it retained the core of the earlier creed of Nicaea, which itself was essentially an Asian creed, as mentioned. Secondly, the main addition was the section on the holy Spirit and this was the result of an eastern and partly Asian controversy, that involving the Pneumatomachi or Macedonians. Macedonius was a priest in Constantinople and bishop of the city intermittently from 344 until his final deposition in 360 and he became the leader of the party that denied full divinity to the holy Spirit: 'Pneumatomachi' meaning 'enemies of the Spirit', a name given to them by their opponents. The party was based around Constantinople and neighbouring areas on both sides of the Bosphorus. Another important leader of the party was Eleusius, bishop of Cyzicus on the Asian side of the sea of Marmara. As with Nicaea I, surviving *acta* for Constantinople I are lacking and therefore it is difficult to speak with certainty about why changes were made to the creed. Nevertheless it seems clear that the much fuller treatment of the holy Spirit, asserting her divinity and equality with Father and Son, was added as a result of the controversy, to refute the Macedonians.[12]

Asia, moreover, cannot be blamed for the only later change to the creed, the infelicitous addition of the 'Filioque' clause (meaning, 'and from the Son'), asserting that the Spirit proceeds from the Son as well as from the Father. It was introduced without the consent of the eastern church or that of an ecumenical council. Its origins are unambiguously in the West, first in sixth century Spain, crucially in the profession of faith issued by the third council of Toledo in 589, then in the realms of Charlemagne in the eighth and ninth centuries, in both cases

---

[12]Kelly, *Creeds*, pp. 296-344; Hanson, *Search for the Christian Doctrine*, op. cit., pp. 791-823; Ortiz de Urbina, *Nicée et Constantinople*, pp. 182-205.

in order to counter residual Arianism, and later with papal support throughout the West.[13]

Ephesus

The third ecumenical council, Ephesus in 431, brings us to the controversy between the schools of Antioch and Alexandria regarding Christ's humanity and divinity.[14] Antioch lies squarely in Asia, in Turkey today, and had a long-standing tradition as an intellectual centre of the early Church, culminating with Theodore of Mopsuestia, the theologian and biblical exegete who died in 428 three years before the beginning of the council. As well as an intellectual centre, the city was one of the four great sees or patriarchates of the early Church, alongside Rome, Constantinople and Alexandria. The exact relationship between Theodore and Nestorius, who was the immediate cause of the council of Ephesus, is unclear. Nestorius was a native of Syria and became a monk in Antioch, where he probably studied under Theodore; certainly he regarded Theodore as his inspiration. After succeeding as bishop of Constantinople in 428, Nestorius soon began to attack the custom of giving Mary the title of 'Theotokos' (*Theotokos* = Mother of God), which had a long and popular tradition in many places and especially in the city of Alexandria.

Alexandria is in Egypt and therefore an African city. Yet at the time we are considering its situation in the eastern, Greek-speaking half of the Roman empire was more central to its identity than being in Africa. As its name suggests, the city had been founded by the Greek emperor Alexander the Great in the

[13] Kelly, *Creeds*, pp. 358-67.

[14] For the council of Ephesus and the schools of Antioch and Alexandria see: Grillmeier, *Christ*, i, pp. 443-87; Jedin, *History*, ii, pp. 93-111; H. Chadwick, *The Church in Ancient Society: From Galilee to Gregory the Great* (Oxford University Press, 2001), pp. 515-39.

fourth century BC and it looked eastwards, into the Greek-speaking and Asian worlds much more than westwards. Even after Hecateaus, who included all of Africa within Asia, as mentioned, some geographers regarded the river Nile and its delta as the border between Asia and Africa, and included Alexandria within Asia because it lay within the delta area, albeit on the western edge. Alexandria had an even older and richer intellectual tradition, both Christian and otherwise, than Antioch.

How far East and into Asia can we push both Antioch and Alexandria? I am far from being an expert on this important topic and the issues involved often seem elusive, though considerable research has been done on them and more clearly needs to be. We know something about the connections between early Christianity and the religions of the East, even though the new Testament says little about them, and it is clear that links continued into the time of the council of Ephesus and beyond, even though Christians seem to have been keen, on the whole, to preserve the distinctiveness of their religion and to present in as uncontaminated by other religions. It is noticeable that the most influential and implacable 'Nestorians', at least in the eyes of the Alexandrians at the second ecumenical council of Constantinople in 553, as we shall see, all came from further East: Theodore, bishop of Mopsuestia, mentioned above, Theodoret, bishop of Cyrrhus in Syria, and Ibas, bishop of Edessa, who takes us into the Persian world. The remarkable spread of the Syriac (Nestorian) church into Persia and central Asia, Tibet and China, also shows an eastern and Asian orientation. In south-east Asia, there are signs of Syriac Christian presence in the Malay-Indonesian region in the seventh century.[15] Peter Brown and S. Lieu have urged us to

---

[15]B. Colless, 'The Traders of the Pearl: The Mercantile and Missionary Activities of Persian and Armenian Christians in South-East Asia', Part 2 'The

think of a more eastern centre to early Christianity through their studies of Manichaeism, which must be seen within a Christian context. Mani (executed in 274/7) came from southern Mesopotamia and spoke of himself as belonging to the 'land of Babylon'. He claimed to be an apostle of Jesus Christ and his movement was described as a 'Christian heresy' by Ambrosiaster in the early fourth century. Eusebius of Caesarea, writing about the same time, also saw the movement, which he described as 'a poisonous snake entering the Roman world from barbarous Persia', as much influenced by Christianity. It became a form of 'crypto-Christianity'. The early centre of the movement lay on the borders of the Roman and Persian empires and from there it spread both eastwards as far as China and westwards into many parts of the Roman empire, often following the routes of the silk trade, as Lieu has pointed out.[16]

Malay Peninsula', *Abr-Nahrain*, ix (1969-70), pp. 105 ff.

[16] P.R. Brown, 'The Diffusion of Manichaeism in the Roman Empire', *Journal of Roman Studies*, lix (1969), pp. 92-103, reprinted in his, *Religion and Society in the Age of Saint Augustine* (London, 1972), pp. 94-118 (see especially pp. 97, 106-7 and 110). Of the many works by S.N.C. Lieu on Manichaeism, see especially, *Manichaeism in the Later Roman Empire and Medieval China* (Manchester University Press, 1985), and *Manichaeism in Central Asia and China* (Leiden: Brill, 1998), see especially pp. xx-xxi and 204-7.

On Christianity in Asia, see also: J.S. Trimingham, *Christianity among the Arabs in Pre-Islamic Times* (London and Beirut: Longmans and Librarie du Liban, 1975 and 1990); Leslie W. Brown, *The Indian Christians of St Thomas: An Account of the Ancient Syrian Church of Malabar* (2nd edn., Cambridge University Press, 1982); A.M. Mundadan, *History of Christianity in India*, vol. 1, *From the Beginning up to the Middle of the Sixteenth Century* (Bangalore: Church History Association of India, 1984, reprinted 1989); R. Le Coz, *L'Église d'Orient: Chrétiens d'Irak, d'Iran et de Turquie* (Paris: Cerf, 1995); J.M. Fiey, *Communautés Syriaques en Iran et Irak des Origines à 1552* (London, Variorum Reprints, 1979); S.H. Moffett, *A History of Christianity in Asia*, vol. 1, *Beginnings to 1550* (San Francisco: Harper, 1992; revised edn., Maryknoll: Orbis, 1998); I. Gillman and Hans-Joachim Klimkeit, *Christians in*

Alexandria was a great metropolis whose trading links were principally eastwards, certainly as far as India. It therefore seems likely that its intellectuals had some knowledge, however imperfect, of the Hindu scriptures, of Buddhism, and of the other great religions of the East. One of the Antiochene school's criticisms of Mary's title of 'Mother of God' was that it seemed to compromise Christianity too much with the pagan religions of Egypt and the East, to make of her a goddess.

The council of Ephesus may appear a defeat for Asian theology (Antioch) at the hands of Africa (Alexandria). Nestorius was condemned and deposed as bishop of Constantinople, Cyril of Alexandria and Mary's title of 'Theotokos' were vindicated. But this is an over-simplification. First, because Antiochene theology recovered the initiative, notably at the subsequent councils of Chalcedon and Constantinople III. Secondly, there was the rapid and extensive spread of Christianity eastwards through the Nestorian churches, though sadly they lost communion with the main body of the Church. And thirdly, because Alexandria must be seen as a city of the eastern empire in close contact with the world of Asia.

Chalcedon

Chalcedon, the place of the fourth ecumenical council, also lies in Asia.[17] Renaming means that the town, once a neighbour of Constantinople, on the southern shore of the Bosphorus, is today a suburb of Istanbul called Kadiköy. The

---

Asia before 1500 (Richmond: Curzon Press, 1999); Martin Palmer, *The Jesus Sutras: Rediscovering the Lost Religion of Taoist Christianity* (London: Piatkus, 2001). I thank Dr. Anthony O'Mahony of Heythrop College, London, for most of these references.

[17]For Chalcedon see: Grillmeier, *Christ*, i, pp. 543-57; Jedin, *History*, ii, pp. 114-21; *Decrees*, i, pp. 75-6 and 83-7. Chadwick, *Church in Ancient Society*, op. cit., pp. 570-83.

Asian nature of the council is reinforced by the provenance of the bishops attending – the overwhelming majority were from the East, the large majority from Asia, as mentioned – and by its endorsement of the Antiochene teaching of two distinct natures in Christ, human and divine, against the monophysitism of Alexandria. The council's 'Definition of Faith', in which this and the earlier teaching of Nicaea I, Constantinople I and Ephesus was set out, is perhaps the most authoritative and influential statement of the Church outside of the Scriptures. It was the seal of doctrinal development in the early Church and has remained a guiding principle for most Christian churches ever since.

Chalcedon was crucial, too, for authority in the Church. It defined the status and the list of ecumenical councils and thereby established ecumenical councils as the most important institution for the Church's future development. Before Chalcedon, Nicaea I was recognised as special and of universal authority, even though it was not always referred to as 'ecumenical'; but Constantinople I was seen rather as a local eastern synod and the status of the controversial council of Ephesus was still much debated. Chalcedon, in its 'Definition of Faith', mentioned these and only these three previous councils, giving them the title of 'ecumenical', which henceforth became a technical term for councils representing the whole Church and therefore of universal authority, as distinct from regional, diocesan and other councils with only a limited mandate. Nicaea I was confirmed again, Constantinople I was effectively promoted to the status of an ecumenical council because its revised version of the Nicene creed was endorsed for the whole Church, and the disputed council of Ephesus was approved. Some other candidates for ecumenicity, moreover, were ruled out, either explicitly or implicitly. In particular, the decisions of the so-called 'Robber council' of Ephesus, or Ephesus II, held in 449, were overturned.

The predominantly Asian complexion of the council of Chalcedon wrecks the argument that theology and church order have been imposed upon the universal Church by the West. On the contrary, they were given to the Church, in this crucial council, principally by Asia.

Constantinople II and III

The fifth and sixth ecumenical councils, Constantinople II in 553 and Constantinople III in 680-1, follow on from Chalcedon. They continued the debate about Christ's humanity and divinity. Constantinople II saw a reversal for the school of Antioch inasmuch as the main act of the council was to condemn three leading Anthiochene theologians, Theodore of Mopsuestia, Theodoret of Cyrrhus and Ibas of Edessa, mentioned earlier. The condemnation, known as 'The Sentence Against the Three Chapters', was imposed upon the council and pushed through by the emperor Justianian, against the better judgement of most church leaders, including pope Vigilius, especially because all three men were long since dead and the previous council of Chalcedon had chosen not to condemn them. In this sense the council cannot be said to represent the wisdom of the whole Church. Justinian's aim was to placate the monophysites of Egypt and to regain their loyalty to the empire and in this, sadly, he was unsuccessful as the Coptic church continued on its path into schism.[18]

Constantinople III, however, confirmed Chalcedon and continued further in the Antiochene direction. It rejected the monothelite tendency of the Alexandria school, which taught a single will in Christ in accordance with his one nature and one

---

[18]*Decrees*, i, pp. 107-13; Grillmeier, *Christ*, ii, part 2, pp. 438-62.

person or hypostasis, and affirmed instead two wills, one human and the other divine, following Christ's two natures as Son of God and Son of man.[19] The two most important theologians who prepared the way for the teaching of the council had strong Asian connections: Sophronius, patriarch of Jerusalem (634-8), who was born in Damascus and lived for some years in a monastery in Jerusalem before he became patriarch; and Maximus the Confessor (580-662), a disciple of Sophronios who lived in his entourage for a time and was born, according to the biography by his contemporary George of Resaina (a hostile source but concrete in detail), near lake Tiberias in Galilee, the son of a Samaritan merchant and a Persian slave girl.[20]

Nicaea II

Nicaea II in 787, the last of the councils recognised as ecumenical by both East and West, turned to another topic, religious art. In this case, too, both the controversy and the solution came principally from Asia. Thus, almost all the leading figures on both sides of the controversy came from Asia Minor (modern Turkey) or Syria: notably the Byzantine rulers of the Isaurian dynasty, most of whom were iconoclasts except for the empress Irene, who played a decisive role in the iconophile victory at the council. There was an iconoclast movement in seventh century Armenia and in the early eight century several bishops in Asia Minor, notably Constantine of Nakoleia and Thomas of Claudiopolis, condemned the veneration of images. The council of Hieria in 754, the high point in iconoclast fortunes, was held in Asia, in the palace of Hieria near Chalcedon. On the iconophile side, its leading theologian John Damascene (c.675-749/54) was born in Damascus in Syria and became a monk in St Sabas monastery near Jerusalem where he

---

[19]*Decrees*, i, pp. 124-130.

[20]See *EEC* and *ODB* under 'Sophronius' and 'Maximus the Confessor'.

wrote his treatises. The source of the controversy, moreover, lay partly in other religions with Asian origins: Manichaeism, discussed earlier, according to which anything material -- therefore all art, including religious art -- was seen as part of the evil principle; also Judaism and Islam, with their abhorrence of any representation of the divine. Iconoclasts were influenced by these arguments and by a desire not to offend Jews and Muslims in the hope – still alive in the eighth century – that they might convert *en masse* to Christianity. The council, however, voted to defend religious art and so ensured another gift of inestimable value from Asia to the universal Church.[21]

Western Influence in a Minor Key

Another way of looking at the predominantly eastern and Asian contribution to the first seven ecumenical councils is through the relative paucity of the contribution from the West. Confirmation of the councils' decrees by the pope, the bishop of Rome, was important – indeed essential alongside that of the other patriarchal sees -- but in terms of theological input the West played a minor role. The possible influence of Tertullian and Ossius of Cordoba upon 'homoousios' in the creed of Nicaea has been mentioned but this seems about the limit of western influence upon the creed. There is no evidence of a western contribution to the revised version of the creed produced by the first council of Constantinople in 381. Regarding the council of Ephesus, pope Celestine I's support for Cyril of Alexandria, against Nestorius, before, during and after the council was important to the outcome but the theological controversy was essentially eastern. It is perhaps symptomatic that Augustine of Hippo, the greatest theologian of the West in the early Church, was invited to the council of Ephesus but died before the invitation reached him! At Chalcedon there was a

---

[21]*ODB*, ii, pp. 975-7 'Iconoclasm'; *Decrees*, i, pp. 133-7.

more direct theological contribution from the West, the 'Tome' or letter that pope Leo I wrote to Flavian archbishop of Constantinople. The long letter provided a theological resource for Chalcedon's 'Definition of Faith' and this was acknowledged in the Definition. On the other hand, the council assembled, at the insistence of the empress Pulcheria, against the wishes of pope Leo, who considered his letter to Flavian to be sufficient to resolve the dispute and therefore judged the council to be unnecessary. The council, moreover, promulgated the Definition as its own document even while it acknowledged Leo's Tome as an important contribution to it.[22]

Constantinople II was convened by the emperor Justinian against the better judgement of pope Vigilius, as mentioned earlier, and the western contribution to the council was small. The role of the West in both Constantinople III and Nicaea II was more significant inasmuch as the popes of the time and the majority of the western church supported the teachings that were endorsed by the two councils. Pope Agatho's legates played a leading role in the conduct of Constantinople III and pope Hadrian I supported empress Irene in her summoning the second council of Nicaea in 787 and her conduct of it. Both councils, nevertheless, were dealing with theological controversies whose foci and solutions lay primarily within the eastern church and only very secondarily in the western.[23]

Mentality of the Decrees

A final point is that the mentality of the councils' decrees, it seems to me, is more eastern than western. Sometimes it is argued that the councils imposed upon the universal church a mentality that is rigid, analytic and abstract, typically western.

---

[22]Jedin, *History*, ii, pp. 103-7 and 114-21; *Decrees*, i, pp. 83-7.

[23]Jedin, *History*, ii, pp. 457-8 and 634-5, and iii, pp. 34-36.

Yet a closer look at the decrees suggests almost the opposite. Here we return to the knotty question of whether Greek thought, which certainly much influenced the decrees, was more eastern or western. In two respects, it seems to me, the decrees reveal an eastern face.

First, they display a cyclical view of life more than the linear and developing one traditionally associated with the West. This reflection strikes me, yet I do not have the knowledge to back it up properly, so it is left with you unexplored.

Secondly, there is space and flexibility within the language of the decrees. Here I feel confident to say a little more. This space and flexibility in the language means that the decrees are better seen as signposts pointing to open fields and mountains, warning too of false trails, rather than as the batons of policemen herding people into prisons – as sometimes they are portrayed and hence rejected in the cause of liberation from western colonial theology. There seems to me an inbuilt breadth within the Greek languge – I hesitate to say 'poeticness' – somewhat in contrast to the more precise, legal and pragmatic Latin of the West. One only has to look up in a dictionary the three words that Christians eventually settled upon in expressing the mysteries of the Trinity and the Incarnation to see how elastic they are: 'ousia' (οὐσία) for the one 'being' of God, 'hupostasis' (ὑπόστασις) for 'person' as in the three persons of the Trinity, and 'phusis' (Φύσις) for 'nature' as in the human and divine natures of Christ. The meanings of 'hupostasis', according to Liddell & Scott's standard *Greek-English Lexicon*, are as follows: standing under, supporting, sediment, jelly or thick soup, duration, coming into existence, origin, foundation, substructure, argument, confidence, courage, resolution, steadiness, promise, substantial nature, substantial existence, reality, wealth, property, and various others! A similarly broad range of meanings will be found under 'ousia' and 'phusis'.

There is, too, much overlap between the three words. To regard them as expressing rigidly defined concepts is manifestly wrong: there is plenty of space within them to accommodate most theological approaches.

Another reason for what might be called the 'accommodation' of the decrees is the principle of unanimity. Ecumenical councils are not like parliaments in England -- my own country -- or most national assemblies in the West today, where a majority of one is sufficient to pass a law. Rather, in these councils unanimous consent, or virtual unanimity, has traditionally been required for approval. At the first council of Nicaea in 325 all but two bishops agreed to the creed and the principle of unanimity remained in force subsequently even if it often proved difficult to achieve. As a result, especially in doctrinal statements, formulas had to be found that were sufficiently elastic to accommodate the views or all, or almost all, sections of opinion. This was helped, in the councils of the early Church, by the fluidity of the Greek language itself, as mentioned.

In the Nicene creed, to take but one example, the crucial word 'homoousios' (ὁμοούσιος, of the same being), to express the Son's relationship with the Father, could be and was interpreted in various ways. The search for harmony and consensus has always seemed to me a quality of the East more than of the West, another gift of Asia to the universal Church flowing from the first seven ecumenical councils.

Chapter 2: Middle Ages and Trent

This second lecture examines the long period in the middle of the Church's history: principally what is traditionally called the Middle Ages; then also the very important council of Trent in the sixteenth century, and its aftermath. If the Middle Ages is taken in a narrow sense, from the point of view of conciliar history, as beginning with the schism between the churches of East and West in the eleventh century and continuing until the eve of the Reformation in the sixteenth century, it amounts to some five hundred years or a quarter of the Church's history. During this time there were ten general councils of the western church: the four Lateran councils in Rome in 1123, 1139, 1179 and 1215, two councils in Lyons in France in 1245 and 1274, the council of Vienne, also in France, in 1311-12, the council of Constance in Germany in 1414-18, the council held first in Basel in Switzerland and then transferred to Florence in Italy, which lasted from 1431 to 1445, and finally the fifth Lateran council in Rome from 1512-17. If the council of Trent is included, and remembering that there were long gaps without ecumenical (or general) councils both before the first Lateran council in 1123 and after the council of Trent, then the span is a millennium: half the Church's history squeezed into this lecture, from after the second council of Nicaea II in 787 -- or from 871 if the disputed fourth council of Constantinople in 869-70 is included – until some three centuries after the conclusion of Trent, the opening of the first Vatican council in 1869.

Status of the Councils

The first question to be asked concerns the status of these eleven councils. Are they to be considered ecumenical councils or, rather, general councils of the western (or Roman Catholic) church? It is, clearly, a very important question inasmuch as upon the answer hangs the authority to be given to conciliar statements during this long period when the centre of the Church moved to the West. They are not, of course, regarded as ecumenical by the Orthodox Church, the oriental (orthodox) churches and the churches of the Reformation. The Orthodox Church accept as ecumenical only the first seven councils from Nicaea I to Nicaea II in 787, as mentioned in the last lecture, and does not extend the list to include the medieval councils for the obvious reason that it was not represented at them in any full sense. The oriental (orthodox) churches vary in their attitude to the early councils but they agree with the Orthodox church regarding the medieval ones. The churches of the Reformation vary in their attitude towards the authority of councils as a whole, stressing rather the authority of Scripture, and none of them, it seems clear, would extend the list of ecumenical councils beyond Nicaea II, both because subsequent councils lacked the participation of the eastern church and because the churches of the Reformation tend to reject the authority of the medieval church in general, and therefore its councils, on the grounds that it was in a state of radical error.

What about the attitude of the Roman catholic church? The answer is not simple. Medieval people themselves, in western Christendom, were uncertain about the status of their own councils and the weight of opinion appears to have been that they were not ecumenical. The point is brought out most clearly in the profession of faith that the council of Constance in 1417 required of a future pope. In listing the councils that the pope should respect, the profession drew a distinction between the eight 'holy universal/ecumenical' (Latin, *universalia*) councils from Nicaea I to Constantinople IV and the subsequent 'general' (Latin, *generalia*) councils of the medieval West, the 'general councils at the Lateran, Lyons and Vienne', as it called them.[24] The distinction between ecumenical and general councils was not expanded upon but it is evident that some difference in status was intended. Other evidence, mainly from the fifteenth and early sixteenth centuries, showing that the medieval councils were not then usually regarded as ecumenical, has been summarised by Victor Peri and Luis Bermejo.[25] It was thought impossible to have an ecumenical council without the participation of the eastern church.

The move to promote the medieval councils to ecumenical status came about during the Counter-Reformation. Catholic apologists sought to defend the true church as they saw it, against the attacks of the Reformation, by an appeal to its medieval heritage. The ten councils from Lateran I to Lateran V formed an important part of this heritage. Influential in this development were Robert Bellarmine, the Jesuit theologian, and Cesare Baronius, the Oratorian scholar, both cardinals, and the so-called 'Roman edition' of the councils, which was published in four volumes in 1608-12 under the title, *Τῶν ἁγίων οἰκουμενικῶν συνόδων τῆς καθολικῆς ἐκκλησίας παντα: Concilia generalia ecclesiae catholicae Pauli V pontificis maximi auctoritate edita.*

This monumental edition, produced by scholars working in Rome under the auspices of pope Paul V (hence its name 'the Roman edition'), attempted to decide which councils the Roman catholic church regarded as ecumenical (or general) and which

---

[24]*Decrees*, i, p. 442.

[25]V. Peri, 'Il numero dei concili ecumenici nella tradizione cattolica moderna', *Aevum*, 37 (1963), pp. 473-5; L. Bermejo, *Church, Conciliarity and Communion* (Anand: Gujarat Sahitya Prakash, 1990), pp. 77-8.

were the decrees legitimately promulgated by them and therefore binding upon Christians. It gave to the ten medieval councils the same status as those of the early church, calling them all 'ecumenical' in the Greek part of the book's title and 'general' in the Latin part, thus cunningly sliding over the possible distinction between the two words. It included nineteen councils: the seven generally accepted councils of the undivided church from Nicaea I to Nicaea II, Constantinople IV, the ten medieval councils from Lateran I to Lateran V (excluding the Basel part of Basel-Florence) and Trent. This list came to be widely accepted within the Roman catholic church and 'ecumenical' rather than 'general' became the preferred term for the councils. The list gained a semi-official status, though the issue was never defined in an authoritative way.[26]

The issue was reopened in recent times. The year 1974 saw two important contributions. First, the influential Dominican theologian Yves Congar wrote a wide-ranging article on criteria for ecumenicity in councils, in which he questioned the list of twenty-one ecumenical councils (the nineteen from Nicaea I to Trent plus Vatican I and II) that had become traditional within the Roman catholic church.[27] Secondly, as part of the celebrations of the seventh centenary of the second council of Lyons in 1274, pope Paul VI wrote a letter to cardinal Willebrands, president of the Secretariat for Christian Unity, in which he referred to this and the earlier medieval councils as 'general councils of the West' (*generales synodos in occidentali orbe*) rather than as ecumenical councils: a choice of language

---

[26]Tanner, *Councils*, pp. 7-8 and 49-50.

[27]Y. Congar, 'Structures ecclésiales et conciles dans les relations entre Orient et Occident', *Revue des sciences philosophiques et théologiques*, 58 (1974), pp. 355-90. See also the earlier article of V. Peri, mentioned in the previous footnote but one.

that is significant and appears intended.[28] Since then there has been some further discussion of the issue, though not as much as might have been expected in view of its possible fruitfulness. There has been a general tendency even within the Roman catholic communion of follow the lead of Paul VI and call the medieval councils 'general councils of the western church' rather than cling to the ecumenical title for them. The Anglican-Roman Catholic International Commission (ARCIC) touched briefly on the issue in its first 'Agreed Statement on Authority in the Church' (1976), no. 19, mentioning obliquely the distinction between ecumenical and general councils, but unfortunately it did not develop the point.

Even if the medieval councils are seen as general councils of the western church, rather than as fully ecumenical councils, they remain, of course, of great significance. They were the most authoritative councils in western Christendom and it was in western Christendom that the large majority of Christians then lived: perhaps 60 million of the total christian population of around 80 million in the year 1300, to make a very rough guess . Certainly there was still vitality in the eastern church and councils continued there into the modern era: for example, the councils of Constantinople in 1341 and 1351, which endorsed Hesychasm, and the councils of Jassy in 1642 and Jerusalem in 1672, which taught concerning the eucharist and the nature of the church. If this lecture were properly developed, it would include a consideration of Asian influences upon these councils. With the advance of Islam, however, the Orthodox Church was for the most part a church on the defensive and developments were limited. Islam's continuing dominance of north Africa, moreover, meant there was, sadly, only a small contribution from Christianity in this region. The mainstream of life and

---

[28]*Acta Apostolicae* Sedis, 66 (1974), p. 620.

development in the church moved westwards and the general councils of the western church formed the central core of conciliar development. When a schism occurs, as between the churches of East and West in the eleventh century, the clock cannot simply be stopped until the wound is healed: development continues even within a fragmented situation. Another obvious point is that the Church before the schism between East and West was far from fully united: there were major and enduring schisms after the councils of Ephesus and Chalcedon, for example, as well as many others. The Church has never been fully united, except perhaps for an hour after Pentecost! Councils, whether ecumenical or general, have always been held in fragmented situations: they represent at best, both in the early Church and in the Middle Ages, the mainstream of Christian tradition rather than the fullness of unity. In this sense the medieval councils are not so markedly different from those of the first millennium.

Nevertheless there is a difference and one that is important to our concerns. Hence this rather long excursus on the status of medieval councils. The difference between the early and the medieval councils, the lesser status of the latter, is important first because it means the Church today is not so definitively bound to its medieval and subsequent developments, more able to return to its Asian roots, than is often suggested. The point was made succinctly by Cardinal Ratzinger some years ago when he stated that in any reunion with the eastern orthodox churches, nothing would be expected of them that went beyond the *status quo* at the time of the beginning of the schism in the eleventh century.[29] It is important, secondly, because medieval people's

---

[29] J. Ratzinger, *Principles of Catholic Theology* (San Francisco: Ignatius Press, 1987), pp. 198-200 (lecture originally delivered in Graz, Austria, in 1976). He later drew back somewhat from the conclusion: *Church,*

perception of the lesser status of their own councils seems to have resulted in an unwillingness on the part of these councils to move beyond their Asian past in doctrinal matters. The councils issued relatively few decrees of a doctrinal nature, said little that was new; their focus was on church order.

Little Development in Doctrine

The relative lack of decrees of a doctrinal nature enacted by the medieval councils is immediately evident. The first three councils in question, Lateran I in 1123, Lateran II in 1138 and Lateran III in 1179, issued no decrees of a doctrinal nature: all those enacted are of a disciplinary or moral nature, touching on the behaviour of clergy and laity and various issues of church order.[30] Of the seventy-one canons promulgated by the fourth Lateran council in 1215, all but two are likewise of a disciplinary rather than a doctrinal nature. The two exceptions are the first two decrees, entitled respectively 'The catholic faith' and 'The error of abbot Joachim'. The first decree contains a creed, aimed principally at the Cathars, who constituted the most serious heresy of the time. It comes closest in form to the great doctrinal statements of the early councils. In style, however, it is cumbersome, almost tortuous, and it never replaced the creeds of Nicaea I and Constantinople I, nor indeed does it seem to have had a major influence even in the medieval period. The final paragraph of the decree contains the statement, 'There is one universal church of the faithful outside of which nobody at all is saved', and the first mention in an ecumenical or general council of transubstantiation to describe Christ's

---

Ecumenism and Politics (Slough: St Paul Publications, 1988), pp. 80-3.

[30]*Decrees*, i, pp. 187-225. The distinction between doctrine and discipline or morals is used here in a common sense way, bearing in mind that they cannot be entirely separated.

presence in the eucharist: 'His body and blood are truly contained in the sacrament of the altar under the forms of bread and wine, the bread and wine having been changed in substance (*transubstantiatis*), by God's power, into his body and blood.' These two declarations are important exceptions to the present argument. They have certainly had a major influence upon ecclesiology and the doctrine of the eucharist in the western church. The second decree of Lateran IV, entitled 'The error of abbot Joachim', is, however, of historical rather than theological interest. The 'error' of Joachim was not a theological heresy on his part, rather, as the council saw it, his unfairly accusing Peter Lombard, author of the *The Sentences*, of heresy regarding the Trinity. The decree is a defence of Peter Lombard more than a condemnation of the abbot.[31]

The next council, Lyons I in 1245, which was summoned by the canonist pope Innocent IV, concerned itself mainly with issues of canon law, the deposition of the emperor Frederick II, and the crusade. There were no decrees of a doctrinal nature.[32] Lyons II in 1274, likewise, concerned itself with canon law and the crusade.[33] It also witnessed a fleeting reunion with (part of) the Orthodox Church through the Byzantine emperor, Michael VIII Palaeologus. The profession of faith that Rome asked the emperor Michael to make is an important theological statement, especially regarding the main issues in dispute between East and West, namely the procession of the holy Spirit, purgatory, the seven sacraments, and papal authority. The profession, however, was never promulgated by the council and so is not, strictly speaking, a decree of the council.[34] It was, moreover, quickly

---

[31] Ibid., i, pp. 230-71.

[32] Ibid., i, pp. 278-301.

[33] Ibid., i, pp. 309-31.

[34] J. Neuner and J. Dupuis (eds.), *The Christian Faith in the Doctrinal*

rejected by the Orthodox Church as a whole and may be seen principally as a statement of the western rather than the universal church. Like St Augustine's death before Ephesus, Thomas Aquinas, the greatest of all theologians of the medieval West, died on his way to the council.

Vienne in 1311-12, the next council, issued one doctrinal decree on some rather obscure theological controversies about the soul being the form of the body, both in Christ and in ourselves, and about the effects of baptism. Its other forty-five decrees concerned the sorry business of the suppression of the order of Knights Templar, the crusade, and various matters of canon law and church order.[35] The council of Constance (1414-18) was dominated by its healing of the schism caused by the three claimants to the papacy. It also made, however, important theological statements in its condemnations of the English and Czech theologians, John Wyclif and John Hus.[36] The council of Basel, which saw itself as continuing the uncompleted work of Constance, became embroiled in an unsuccessful struggle for sovereignty with pope Eugenius IV and its main other preoccupation was with various practical reforms of the Church.

When pope Eugenius 'transferred' the council of Basel to the city of Florence in Italy, against the wishes of the majority, who remained at Basel, this new council was responsible for decrees of reunion with the Orthodox Church and with groups of Armenians, Copts, Syrians, Chaldeans and Maronites.[37] All these decrees contained important theological statements and the

---

Documents of the Catholic Church (2nd edn., London: Collins, 1983), pp. 16-20.

[35] *Decrees*, i, pp. 336-401, and ii, pp. 1150-1.

[36] Ibid., i, pp. 411-16 and 421-31.

[37] Ibid., i, pp. 523-8, 534-59, 567-83 and 586-90.

very detailed decree of reunion with the Armenians, especially its treatment of the seven sacraments, anticipated much of Trent and had an enduring influence upon Roman Catholic theology. On the other hand, they only had very limited ecumenical success. The reunion was not 'received' by the Orthodox Church and in the other cases only small groups within the churches were reunited with the Roman Catholic church. The decrees are best seen as influential within the Roman Catholic church rather than as of major importance for the universal Church. The limited authority of the council, even within the Catholic church, is illustrated by its extreme declaration of the impossibility of salvation outside the Church, which has proved an embarrassment also to Catholics and has effectively been rejected, and by its teaching on the sacrament of ordination which was overturned by pope Pius XII. On salvation it said in the decree of reunion with the Copts:

> '[The council] firmly believes, professes and preaches that all those who are outside the catholic church, not only pagans but also Jews or heretics and schismatics, cannot share in eternal life and will go into the everlasting fire which was prepared for the devil and his angels, unless they are joined to the catholic church before the end of their lives.'[38]

Regarding the sacrament of ordination, the council declared the following in its decree of reunion with the Armenians:

> 'The matter [of the sacrament of orders] is the object by whose handing over the order is conferred. So the priesthood is bestowed by the handing over of a chalice

---

[38] Ibid., i, p. 578

with wine and a paten with bread; the diaconate by the giving of the book of the gospels; and the subdiaconate by the handing over of an empty chalice with an empty paten on it.'[39]

Yet pope Pius XII in his apostolic constitution *Sacramentum ordinis* of 1947 abrogated this doctrine or ruling and stated: 'The matter of the holy orders of diaconate, priesthood and episcopate is the laying on of hands alone.'[40]

Finally, for the pre-Reformation period, there is the fifth Lateran council of 1512-17. It enacted a number of decrees concerning a rival council being held at Pisa, reform of the Church, the crusade, and various practical matters, but only one decree of a more strictly theological nature: that supporting the immortality of the soul, seemingly directed against the teaching of the Italian philosopher Pomponazzi.[41]

In summary, it may be said that while the ten general councils of the medieval West, from Lateran I in 1123 to Lateran V in 1512-17, issued some decrees of a doctrinal nature, these were much less numerous and in a minor key compared with those of a disciplinary and practical nature. This is the opposite of the situation during the seven councils of the early Church, from Nicaea I in 325 to Nicaea II in 787, when doctrinal issues predominated over those involving church order. Moreover, the doctrinal statements of these medieval councils largely concerned matters in dispute within the western church: they were not, for the most part, issues of major concern to the wider Church. For the most part, too, the statements were conservative

---

[39]Ibid., i, p. 549.

[40]Neuner and Dupuis, *The Christian Faith*, op. cit., p. 506, no. 1737 (3858).

[41]*Decrees*, i, pp. 595-655 (pp. 605-6 for the doctrinal decree)

in nature; the medieval councils were hesitant to go beyond what the early councils had stated in an authoritative way. This is not at all to say that Christians in the medieval West were uninterested in theology. On the contrary, many indulged in it with passion. It is simply that they did their theology, for the most part, in forums other than general councils: through discussion and books, in monasteries and convents, in schools and universities.

Nevertheless, the fact that the medieval councils were hesitant, in doctrinal matters, to go beyond what the early councils had stated is significant. In these assemblies, which were recognised as more authoritative than the writings of individual theologians or even the collective statements of university faculties, the medieval West lived in awe of its Asian past. The hesitation surely reflects the unease of medieval people regarding the status of their own general councils, which has been dwelt upon earlier. It also reflects a more general sense of western inferiority at this time.

Inferiority Complex of the West

This sense of inferiority is very important to understand. The West today is often accused of promoting an aggressive and domineering form of Christianity. The accusation has come about largely as a result of the expansion of Christianity into a world religion and the self-confidence, frequently arrogance, that accompanied the expansion. It began in the sixteenth century, with the 'discovery of the new world' in western eyes, and developed further with Europe's colonial expansion in the nineteenth and early twentieth centuries. The Middle Ages, however, is before all this. At the time of the medieval councils Christianity had existed for over a millennium and yet seemed to be making little progress. It occupied a small corner of the globe and it knew this: in many ways it was a shrinking religion. That is to say, Christianity, and *a fortiori* western Christendom, was then probably smaller in geographical extent than it had been in the last century of the Roman empire, the time of the early councils. Gains in north and central Europe had been offset by massive losses, mostly to Islam, in the near East and north Africa. Islam, although a much younger religion than Christianity, was already far more widespread, it was already almost a world religion. It continued to advance, except in Spain, and to threaten Christendom, culminating with the capture of Constantinople in 1453. There was also the threat from the north east. Tartars (or Mongols) from central Asia captured Budapest, capital of Hungary, in 1242 and fear remained that they would conquer even further west. The final defeat and extinction of Christianity seemed a real possibility. The first council of Lyons, which was held in 1245, a mere three years after the capture of Budapest, expressed this possibility graphically in its decree relating to the Tartar incursions.

> 'The wicked race of Tartars, seeking to subdue, or rather utterly destroy the christian people, having gathered for a long time past the strength of their tribes, have entered Poland, Russia, Hungary and other christian countries ... As time went on, they could attack stronger christian armies and exercise their savagery more fully upon them. Thus when, God forbid, the world is bereaved of the christian faithful, faith may turn aside from the world to lament its followers destroyed by the barbarity of this people.'[42]

In addition to these physical threats, there was a sense of cultural inferiority. Four cultures or civilizations were thought

---

[42] Ibid., i, p. 297.

to be, in various ways, superior to western Christendom. The first of these was Judaism, a much older religion than Christianity, which possessed in many ways a richer culture and whose people were renowned for their intellectual skills as well as those in business, medicine and other walks of life. The second was Islam, which, as just mentioned, was expanding faster and more widely than Christianity. Its architects and artists were at least as skilled as Christians, as travellers to Spain and the near East could see, and its philosophers, notably Avicenna and Averroës and other commentators on Aristotle, were the envy of western scholars. The third was Byzantium, with its great city of Constantinople, which considered itself, and to some extent was recognised by the West, as the true heir of the ancient world and the early church much more than its upstart neighbours in the West. Finally, the ancient world of Greece and Rome, long since vanished except in Byzantium, yet surviving vigorously in people's memory and still largely unsurpassed by western Christendom in philosophy, literature, art, government and law. In these respects, too, the Middle Ages predates the intellectual self-confidence which became associated with Christianity as it developed into a dominant world religion from the sixteenth century onwards. The underlying mood was rather of unease and defensiveness. Many of the attitudes and responses of the period, which may appear to us today as aggressive and unjustified, such as the crusades, the obsession with heresy, or the attacks on Jews, must be seen in this context. People who are ill at ease or threatened often act in strange ways.

In short, western Christendom in the Middle Ages felt hemmed in both by its neighbours and by its past. In many ways it had never caught up with the age that had gone before it, a strange feeling that we find difficult to appreciate. It had never really caught up with the ancient world of Greece and Rome, nor with the early Church, all of which were profoundly influenced by the eastern and Asian world, as was argued in the first lecture. Now it was threatened, too, both physically and culturally by outside enemies and these also came predominantly from Asia. All this was reflected in the conservatism and relative paucity of doctrinal statements of the medieval councils. The giant of Asia continued to project its powerful presence over the medieval West.

Decrees on Church Order

So much for the doctrinal teaching of the medieval general councils. What about the decrees of a disciplinary nature, those touching church order, which made up the large majority of the councils' business. There is no doubt that the medieval councils moved the western church beyond – many would say, away from – its Asian roots in matters of discipline and church order, in the practice of Christianity. They were partly responsible for major and long-lasting developments on a whole range of issues: many aspects of prayer and popular religion, religious orders, the sacraments, crusades and the inquisition, attitudes towards dissent within the christian community and towards other religions, the papacy and church government. It would, however, be largely anachronistic to claim that the development was consciously in a 'western' direction. Indeed, western self-consciousness is more alleged from outside, by other countries and civilizations, than recognised by the West. From the growth of nation-states in the sixteenth century onwards, until very recently, the countries of the West have thought of themselves primarily as individual countries -- Spain, France, Germany, England, USA, and so on, with their own languages and traditions – rather than as belonging to the western world. But that is another story! It would also be wrong to suggest that medieval developments in the practice of Christianity were conscious departures from the early Church, conscious departures from the Church's Asian foundations. The medieval Church, especially its general councils, always thought of itself as in continuity with the early Church, as developing in time in a legitimate manner. The profession of faith that the council of Constance required of a future pope, mentioned above, expresses the point well, so it may be quoted again and more fully. The pope was to promise:

> '... that as long as I am in this fragile life I will firmly believe and hold the catholic faith, according to the traditions of the apostles, of the general councils and of the other holy fathers, especially of the eight holy ecumenical councils – namely the first at Nicaea, the second at Constantinople, the third at Ephesus, the fourth at Chalcedon, the fifth and sixth at Constantinople, the seventh and Nicaea, and the eighth at Constantinople – as well as of the general councils at the Lateran, Lyons and Vienne, and I will preserve this faith unchanged to the last dot and will confirm, defend and preach it to the point of death and the shedding of my blood, and likewise I will follow and observe in every way the rite handed down of the ecclesiastical sacraments of the catholic church.'[43]

The profession reveals a conservatism in ecclesiastical discipline as well as in doctrine.

It has already been argued that the Church today is less definitively bound to the decrees of the medieval councils because of the lower status of these councils in comparison with those of the early Church. In the case of disciplinary decrees

---

[43] Ibid., i, p. 442.

there is the additional reason that many of them treated of contingent matters and therefore are, in principle, open to change. The same point applies, *mutatis mutandis*, to other decrees of a more practical nature, those concerning devotional life and even ecclesiology.

The contingent and therefore changeable nature of much of the medieval councils' decrees concerning church order has been demonstrated in recent times by the apologies issued by the present pope regarding, among other things, the crusades, the Church's treatment of heretics, including the Inquisition, and christian attitudes towards Jews. On all three issues the medieval general councils enacted hardline decrees, expressing views that have now been largely disowned. Regarding the crusades, the councils from Lateran I in 1123 to Lateran V in 1512-17 issued a series of decrees that made christian defence or recapture of the Holy Land, or its 'liberation' as the decrees preferred to speak, the Church's top priority.[44] The fourth Lateran council of 1215 spoke of the holy war as 'this business of Jesus Christ' (*negotium Jesu Christi*) and excommunicated those who had promised to joint the expedition and then had second thoughts.[45] The same council 'condemned all heretics, whatever names they may go under, for they have different faces indeed but their tails are tied together inasmuch as they are alike in their pride.' It ordered kings and other secular authorities, under pain of excommunication, to expel heretics from their territories, 'to cleanse their lands of this heretical filfth'.[46] This is certainly a form of ethnic, or religious, cleansing that is rightly abhorred

---

[44]Ibid., i, pp. 191-2, 267-71, 297-301, 309-12, 350-4, 609-14 and 650-5; N. Tanner, 'Medieval Crusade Decrees and Ignatius's Meditation on the Kingdom', *The Heythrop Journal*, 31 (1990), pp. 505-15.

[45]*Decrees*, i, p. 268.

[46]Ibid., i, p. 233-4.

today. The council of Vienne in 1311-12, in its decrees on the Inquisition, approved the imprisonment and even torture of suspects.[47] Jews were the subject of a series of restrictive and coercive decrees, especially by the fourth Lateran council, which described them as 'perfidious' and 'blasphemers of Christ'.[48] It is painful to continue. We should, moreover, acknowledge the other, brighter side of the coin: the brilliance and creativity of medieval religion in so many areas of life: liturgy and prayer, charity towards the needy and marginalised, cathedrals and parish churches, religious orders, art and music, and so much else. A frequent corollary of energy and commitment in religion is, sadly, intolerance of nonconformists and outsiders, who seem to threaten the good work. But this is not our main concern in this lecture. The relevant point is that recent rethinking about teaching of the medieval councils that seemed at the time very important and yet appears today as repugnant, indicates that it is right to review the pronouncements of these councils more widely, that the Church has a certain freedom to return to its Asian roots in matters of church order.

Council of Trent

The council of Trent must be treated separately from the medieval councils for the obvious reasons that however long one extends the Middle Ages, it cannot be extended into the mid sixteenth century, several decades after the beginning of the Reformation, and because the council's influence dominated the western Church for another three centuries into the modern era. In addition, the primary concern of Trent was doctrine and in this respect it differed from the medieval councils, which focused mainly on discipline and church order, as mentioned. It

---

[47] Ibid., i, pp. 380-3.
[48] Ibid., i, pp. 265-7.

represented a return to the predominantly doctrinal councils of the early church. The differences, however, should not be exaggerated. Trent is often seen as belonging to the new age of Renaissance and discovery – from a European perspective – of the wider world, of Reformation and Counter-Reformation, yet it should also be seen as the crown of medieval religion. The bishops and theologians of Trent were more influenced by late medieval theology than by the Reformation. In matters of church order, too, Trent was largely in continuity with the councils of the Middle Ages.

How much Asian influence remained at Trent, or does the council represent the decisive moment when the Catholic church became westernized? What has been said about the lesser status of the medieval councils applies *a fortiori* to Trent. That is to say, there was no representation of the Orthodox church nor, in any proper sense, of the Protestant churches of the Reformation. Inasmuch as the teachings of the medieval councils may be open to review, so too those of Trent, and the more western biases may be redressed. .

Trent was eager to connect with the Church's eastern and Asian roots. Its first doctrinal decree proclaimed that 'the creed which the holy Roman church uses as the basic principle on which all who profess the faith of Christ necessarily agree' is the Nicene creed -- that produced by the predominantly eastern and Asian councils of Nicaea I and Constantinople I -- and proceeded to reproduce this creed faithfully, with the one exception of the addition of the *Filioque* clause.[49] Immediately afterwards the council tackled the issue of Scripture and Tradition. Here, too, the council connected with the Church's Asian roots: Jesus Christ, the Asian Jew who is the unique

---

[49]Ibid., ii, p. 662

source of the gospel -- God's good news to us -- and the fulfilment of the prophets of the old Testament, all of whom were Asians. This is how the council expressed it:

> 'Our lord Jesus Christ, the Son of God, first proclaimed with his own lips the gospel, which had in the past been promised by the prophets in the sacred scriptures. Then he bade it be preached to every creature through his apostles as the source of the whole truth of salvation and rule of conduct.'[50]

The council went on to speak of Scripture and tradition. This 'gospel', it said, is contained,

> 'in written books and in unwritten traditions which were received by the apostles from the mouth of Christ, or else have come down to us, handed on as it were from the apostles themselves at the inspiration of the holy Spirit.'[51]

Any suggestion that scripture and tradition are two independent sources, that a western church can alter the Asian scriptures, is unjust to Trent. There is but one primordial source, it says, not two, the gospel proclaimed by Jesus Christ, and in the transmission of this gospel to us scripture and tradition are closely linked. The apostles, moreover, all Asians, had a unique role in tradition. It was they who received the traditions from the mouth of Christ and who handed them on.

The roles of scripture and tradition was the first great controversial issue that Trent tackled. The council asserted the importance of the latter in the face of the almost exclusive emphasis placed upon Scripture by the Protestants of the time.

---

[50] Ibid., ii, p. 663.
[51] Ibid., ii, p. 663.

The second major issue was the role of faith and good works in the work of our justification. Here the eastern/Asian and western/European lines become crossed. The controversy lay within the western Church. The two principal authorities to which the Reformers appealed were the Asian Paul of Tarsus, especially in his letter to the Romans, and Augustine of Hippo, an African who belonged to the Latin-speaking western church. Trent, in its decree on justification, both argued that the Reformers were misrepresenting Paul and Augustine and sought to move the debate beyond the confines of the two men into the wider traditions of the Church both East and West. [52]

Regarding the sacraments and church order, Trent may seem to have confirmed and developed a more consciously western direction. It confirmed the list of seven sacraments, which had become established in the thirteenth century, notably through the profession of faith made by the eastern emperor at the second council of Lyons in 1274, and expanded on the teaching regarding them contained in the council of Florence's decree of reunion with the Armenians.[53] Regarding the status and roles of bishops, priests and religious orders, Trent supported the developments that had taken place in the western Church during the Middle Ages. On the other hand, it saw no hardline endorsement of the Gregorian Reform, the movement named after its most notable leader, pope Gregory VII (1073-85), which is usually seen as the decisive moment when the ecclesiology of the western church diverged from that of the eastern. Thus, Trent promulgated no decree on the papacy – mainly because the pope's authority in relation to councils had

---

[52] Ibid., ii, pp. 671-81.
[53] Neuner and Dupuis, *The Christian Faith*, op. cit., p. 19, no. 28 (860); *Decrees*, i, pp. 540-50, and ii, pp. 684-6, 693-713, 726-8, 732-7, 741-4 and 753-9.

been a contested issue within the Catholic community since the time of the councils of Constance and Basel in the fifteenth century and Trent wisely refrained from reopening these wounds – and its decrees relating to bishops, priests and religious are more concerned with reform and rooting out abuses than with enforcing their authority and jurisdiction.[54] The tone of Trent's ecclesiology is closer to that of the early councils than to subsequent medieval developments.

It is time to leave Trent and conclude this lecture. The council is often seen as a hammer that was used against Protestants and ensured the westernization of the Roman Catholic church for many centuries. This is misleading. The council, in many respects, broadened the Church, made it more catholic, allowed it to escape from the excessive Eurocentrism of some aspects of the Protestant Reformation. The latter was an exclusively European phenomenon and Trent incorporated many of its better insights into its own decrees, especially in the early stages of the council. At the same time it rejected the more extreme forms of individualism and self-righteousness to which the doctrine of justification by faith alone, especially, might be prone and which have often been associated, subsequently, with the western psyche. Trent, in many respects, helped to return the Church to its truly catholic and Asian roots.

---

[54]*Decrees*, ii, pp. 686-9, 714-18, 744-53, 759-73, 776-84 and 784-96.

Chapter 3: Vatican I and II

This third and final lecture looks at the two most recent general councils of the Catholic Church, the first and second Vatican councils. They took place at a time when, for the first time in history, Christianity had become a world religion. What was the Asian contribution to them?

Vatican I

The first Vatican council, which took place in St Peter's basilica in Rome during the eight months between December 1869 and July 1870, will not detain us long. It was from the beginning threatened by the outbreak of war between France and Germany and the withdrawal of the two countries' bishops that would probably result. There was also the danger posed by the Italian army, which had encircled Rome in its quest to conquer the Papal States and complete the reunification of Italy. When the Franco-Prussian War broke out in July 1870 the council was postponed, never to reassemble, and as a result its intended business remained unfinished. Earlier, with the two clouds hanging over its head, the council had agreed to focus on what were seen, at least by pope Pius IX and the Roman curia, the organisers of the council, as the most important issues. Only two decrees, as a result, were promulgated.

The first decree, entitled 'Dogmatic Constitution on the Catholic Faith', treated the relationship between faith and reason. On the one hand it argued for a 'twofold order of knowledge': 'We know at one level by natural reason, at the other level by divine faith.' Though 'faith is above reason, there can never be any real disagreement between faith and reason, since it's the same God who, on the one hand, is the source of revelation and infused faith, and on the other hand has endowed the human mind with the light of reason.' Truth, therefore, is one. 'Not only can faith and reason never be at odds with another but they mutually support each other.'[55] If the 'twofold order' of knowledge is emphasised, western influence comes to mind: the separation of faith and reason in medieval scholasticism and more radically in the eighteenth century Enlightenment. The council may be seen as trying to grapple with this problem of separation – perhaps a false problem – in which western analytic thought had become enmeshed. On the other hand, the oneness and unity of truth, upon which the decree also insists, may be closer to the mentality of Asia, which sees truth under different facets but rejects any dichotomies in it.

Vatican I's second decree, 'On the Church of Christ', known from its opening words as *Pastor aeternus*, is more famous. It was originally intended to be a complete treatise on the Church but the curtailment of the council's business meant that in fact only the papacy was treated, culminating in a fourth and final chapter on papal infallibility. Whether the papacy, as portrayed in the decree, represents more the model of authority in the East than in the West may be debated. The decree did not try to base itself upon any secular models of authority, be they of East or West, rather to expound the existing teaching of the Church as found in Scripture and Tradition. The model of authority, however, is more communal than is often alleged. The decree does not say directly that the pope is infallible. It says, rather, that in certain solemn situations the pope possesses 'the infallibility that the divine Redeemer (Christ) willed his Church to enjoy in defining doctrine concerning faith and morals.'[56] In other words, papal infallibility is placed within the

---

[55] *Decrees*, ii, pp. 808-9.
[56] Ibid., ii, pp. 816.

context of the Church, which, as Vatican II later taught, means 'the people of God'.[57] The pope representing God's people in this way is, perhaps, closer to an eastern model of authority than the more juridical and individual model of authority that has often predominated in the West; though the latter model is also clearly there in the decree, especially in the third chapter entitled 'On the power and character of the primacy of the Roman pontiff'.[58]

In addition to the two decrees, the council issued a 'Profession of Faith', which gave pride of place to the Nicene creed in the revised version produced by the first council of Constantinople in 381.[59] The council thus set itself squarely in this Asian tradition. In a sense, too, the declaration of papal infallibility, the bishop of Rome's concern for the whole Church, is an expression of the universal nature of the Church, a move away from a narrowly western Church. The declaration coincided with the rapid growth of the Church worldwide, in Asia and elsewhere, in the nineteenth century. Initially, moreover, the council intended to treat of other topics concerning Asia, notably the eastern churches and missionary work, but these had to be sacrificed when the council was cut short.[60]

In terms of participants, Vatican I was predominantly European. It has been calculated that of the 1056 individuals who were eligible to attend – mostly diocesan bishops but including vicars apostolic, heads of religious orders, and senior

---

[57] Chapter 2 of Vatican II's decree on the Church, *Lumen gentium*, is entitled 'The people of God'.

[58] *Decrees*, ii, pp. 813-15.

[59] Ibid., ii, p. 802.

[60] Jedin, *History*, viii, p. 323.

officials of the Roman curia – 792 attended at least one session and an average of around 700 were present at any given time. About a third of the 792 came from outside Europe but the large majority of them were of European origin, either missionary bishops or the sons of European families that had settled abroad. Asia was represented by forty or so prelates of eastern-rite churches, mostly from the near East, and a similar number of Latin rite bishops and vicars apostolic, including 16 from India and 15 from China, 3 from Indo-China, 1 (archbishop of Manila) from the Philippines, 2 from Korea, and 4 from Indonesia and the Pacific. While a good number of the eastern-rite bishops were Asians, almost all the Latin rite bishops and vicars apostolic were missionaries from Europe.[61]

Though it cannot be said that the participants from Asia had a major influence upon the council, it was not negligible. Of the 417 speeches delivered at the official debates, 30 were made by representatives of Asia.[62] The nine Melkite bishops who attended, led by their patriarch Gregory Yussef (Jussef) of Antioch, formed a substantial group within the minority party of those opposed to the proclamation of papal infallibility and a number of other eastern-rite bishops, notably among the Chaldaeans, voted with the minority.[63] Most of Asia's representatives, however, especially among those of the Latin-rite, voted with the majority supporting papal infallibility: notable exceptions were half a dozen bishops from China who at least occasionally voted with the minority. Most countries in Asia still came under the authority of Propaganda congregation (*Congregatio de propaganda fidei*) in the Roman curia and their

---

[61] K. Schatz, *Vaticanum I, 1869-70* (Paderborn: Schöningh, 1992-4), ii, pp. 16-17; Jedin, *History*, viii, p. 318.

[62] Schatz, *Vaticanum I*, op. cit., ii, p. 18.

[63] Ibid., ii, pp. 53-4.

bishops were influenced by cardinal Barnabò, who was both prefect of the congregation and a strong supporter of papal infallibility. Two Jesuits, both missionary bishops from Europe working in India, were of some importance within the majority party: the German Meurin, apostolic vicar of Bombay, and the Dutchman Steins, apostolic vicar of Calcutta.[64]

The medieval councils, Trent and Vatican I represent the low point in the general thesis of these Placid Lectures. The influence of Asia was felt much less directly in these councils than in the ecumenical councils of the early Church. It was, nevertheless, far from negligible. To state the obvious, the later councils always saw their foundations as lying in the Asian Jesus Christ and the mainly eastern early Church. In terms of councils, they saw themselves as being in continuity with the predominantly Asian early councils and, with a sense of respect and veneration, were reluctant to move beyond them, at least in matters of doctrine. The healthy presence of Asia continued to loom large, even while the councils moved to Europe and the large majority of participants and immediate concerns were European. At these councils, taken together, Asia had far more impact than any other continent except Europe, much more than Africa or America.

Vatican II

The second Vatican council witnessed a significant increase in the influence of Asia – as indeed of the rest of the non-European world – especially during the latter half of the council. The continent was represented by some 250 of the approximately 2,500 individuals (mainly bishops, both diocesans and their auxiliaries, but also vicars apostolic, heads

---

[64]Schatz, *Vaticanum I*, op. cit., ii, pp. 53-55.

of religious orders and senior officials of the Roman curia) who were full members of the council at any given time. In terms of Catholic population, therefore, Asia was well represented. Some 5% of the world's Catholic population then living in Asia were represented by 10% of the members of the council; figures that are influenced by the fact that many of the bishops in question – though a far smaller proportion than at Vatican I – were missionaries from Europe.[65] What about the importance of the Asian contribution?

Preparation

Soon after the announcement of the forthcoming council by pope John XXIII in January 1959, the Roman curia wrote to all prospective members of the council, and various other individuals and institutions, to request their suggestions. 70% of the bishops and other representatives of Asia responded and duly sent in their suggestions, or '*vota*' as they were called. This was the lowest proportion in any of the five continents except Australasia, where the figure was 69%, and compares with 83% for Africa and 80% for Europe. It represents, nevertheless, a decent response since many Chinese and Vietnamese bishops were effectively subjected to enforced silence by their respective governments.[66]

The enormous variety of peoples within the vast continent of Asia showed itself in a corresponding variety of responses in the *vota*. One obviously cannot speak of a single Asian response. Nevertheless, for the most part individually, the responses are interesting and foreshadow many of the themes that were later to influence the council.

---

[65] Alberigo, *Vatican II*, ii, pp. 171-2.
[66] Ibid., i, p. 100.

Bishops of eastern-rite catholic churches were among the few who refused to follow Rome's directives that they submit their *vota* in Latin, giving them instead in Italian or French: a foreshadowing of the eventual conversion to vernacular languages in the liturgy and other areas of church life as a result of the council. The bishop of Krishnagar in India, Louis La Ravoire Morrow, a Salesian originally from USA, was even more direct, saying that 'the Latin language is no longer a means of unifying the Church.' For the eastern-rite churches the question of language concerned their autonomy, an issue that was to develop further during and after the council. Maximus IV, the Melkite patriarch of Antioch, who was to become a leading figure of the council, touched on the issue of autonomy in a letter he wrote to the pope in August 1959, in the name of all Melkite bishops, in which he objected to the seating-arrangement whereby Oriental patriarchs were to be placed behind cardinals, since this would indicate a lack of respect for their churches and 'the importance of the Churches is signified by precedence.' Indeed, the bishops of all the eastern-rite churches, even those with close ties with Rome, such as the Maronites, emphasised in their responses their distinctiveness, their eastern character, their role in reunion with the Orthodox, and that they were not mere appendices of the Roman church.[67]

Other *vota* revealed varying, sometimes almost contradictory, emphases. The vicar apostolic of Purkowerto in Indonesia anticipated the council's emphasis upon inculturation and regular consultation. He wanted the forthcoming council to be organised according to cultural areas, in seven geographical sections, and advocated a plenary council every fifty years alternating with a worldwide conference every twenty-five years. Bishops from Hong Kong, Formosa and the Philippines,

---

[67]Ibid., i, 102, 125 and 378.

as well as others who had been expelled from China and were now living in Europe, asked for a renewal of the Church's condemnations of Communism, a proposal that was not accepted by the council. In a similar vein, the Japanese cardinal Doi of Tokyo wanted a condemnation of intellectual trends such as existentialism and relativism. The Indian cardinal Gracias of Bombay wanted a reform of the Roman Curia as well as definitions of new dogmas about Mary. The archbishop of Taipei in Formosa wanted the eradication of colonialism in evangelisation and the internationalisation of the Roman curia as well as doctrinal definitions regarding the Mystical body, and Mary as mediatrix and coredemptrix, also condemnations of Communism, atheistic humanism and existentialism in accordance with pope Pius XII's encyclical *Humani Generis*: some of which proposals were at least partly accepted by the council and others rejected. Victor Bazin MEP (Missions Etrangères de Paris), archbishop of Rangoon in Burma, wanted the council to decide whether Buddhism should be regarded as atheistic or rather as an incomplete religion, following theologians such as Daniélou, de Lubac, Guardini and Karrer. He clearly favoured the latter approach, anticipating the cautious openings to non-Christian religions that were to mark the council's decree *Nostra Aetate*.[68]

The theology faculty of the Papal Athenaeum in Pune (then Poona) in India submitted its *votum* urging the Catholic church to more cooperation with Protestants and the eastern churches.

---

[68] Ibid., i, pp. 107, 117 and 128. Fuller accounts of the *vota* from India, China and Japan are to be found in: P. Pulikkan, 'Indian Bishops in the First Session: From a Slow Start to an Emerging Conciliar Ethos', in M. Fattori and A. Melloni (eds.), *Experience, Organisations and Bodies at Vatican II* (Leuven, 1999), pp. 87-95; A.S. Lazzarotto, 'I Vescovi Cinesi al Concilio', in ibid., pp. 70-72; A. Zambarbieri, 'Nota alla Participazione dei Vescovi del Giappone al Vaticano II', in ibid., pp. 126-8.

It wanted a group of young priests to be selected, instructed and trained for the work of reunion. It also urged, with a view to ecumenical progress, that the Christological nature of all Marian dogmas be explained. The Church should promote works of charity and social justice, also a more active participation in the liturgy by explaining the rites and words better, though it asked only for 'certain norms and decrees for the use of modern languages.'[69] Also in India, the meeting of the World Council of Churches (WCC) in Delhi in November to December 1961 had an important bearing on the forthcoming Vatican council. Rome eventually agreed to send 'observers' to the assembly, the first time it had sent delegates with this status to a meeting of WCC. By this action Rome met the conditions set by WCC for the latter to send its own observers to the Vatican council. These observers were to play a considerable role in the council and in its favourable reception by other churches.[70]

First Session, Autumn 1962

An event that was to prove crucial to the outcome of the council was the debate on the elections to the conciliar commissions, which took place at the first working session of the council on Saturday 13 October. Ten commissions[71] would be responsible for guiding the decrees through the council, revising or drafting them anew in the light of the speeches and submissions made by the fathers. Would the members of the commissions be much the same as those of the ten conciliar commissions that had been responsible for the preparation of the council and had been organised around and largely controlled by

---

[69]Pulikkan, 'Indian Bishops', op. cit., pp. 95-6.

[70]Alberigo, *Vatican II*, i, pp. 387-8.

[71]There was also the 'Central Coordinating Commission', which was meant to coordinate the work of the ten commissions.

the congregations and other *dicasteri* of the Roman Curia? The rejection of this eventuality, which began at the fateful session on 13 October, led to the opening up of the commissions to a much wider membership.[72] It was quickly followed, partly as a result, by the rejection of almost all the seventy decrees that the preparatory commissions had submitted. The council then had to start virtually from scratch in drafting new decrees, a process that was eventually to last the full four years of the council. In this situation the conciliar commissions, which were responsible for the drafting and revising, assumed an even greater importance.

What was the representation of Asia on these conciliar commissions? Initially the changes from the preparatory to the conciliar commissions were not so radical. Of the 160 members of the ten commissions -- 16 for each of them -- 57% had been members of the preparatory commissions and 43% were new.[73] To these 160, the pope appointed a further 9 to each commission, a total of 90, of whom 70% had belonged to the preparatory commissions and 30% were new.[74] Europeans were much the largest group, though there were more representatives from the other continents than there had been on the preparatory commissions.[75] Of the elected members, Asia counted about 14 (the figure includes missionary bishops of European origin) and thus came well below America (south and north), with its far larger Catholic population, but above Africa and Australia (Oceania). Of the members nominated by the pope, Asia was similarly well represented in proportion to its Catholic

---

[72]Alberigo, *Vatican II*, ii, pp. 26-30.

[73]Ibid., ii, p. 42.

[74]Ibid., ii, p. 44.

[75]Ibid., ii, p. 42.

population.[76] India was the country in the continent with the largest number: 7 elected and one nominated members.[77] The four *periti* (theologians) from India who, in addition, were assigned to the commissions included Father Placid Podipara CMI. Professor of the Pontifical Oriental Institute in Rome and Consultor of the Roman curia's Congregation for Oriental Churches, he had been a Consultor of the council's Preparatory Commission for the Oriental Churches and was then appointed to the corresponding conciliar commission, remaining on it for the duration of the council.[78] For the key posts in the commissions, namely their presidents, vice-presidents and secretaries, the Armenian cardinal Agagianian, who was both Prefect of the curial congregation 'Propaganda Fidei' and president of the corresponding conciliar commission on Missions, was the only Asian representative. The commissions grew considerably in size and competence during the council and the influence of the theologians (*periti*) assigned to them similarly increased.[79] Asia's contribution to them seems to have kept apace of these developments.

Regarding other organs of the council's government, at the top, under the pope, was the 'Council of Presidents' comprising ten cardinals. Asia was represented by Cardinal Tappouni, patriarch of Antioch, of the Syro-Catholic rite, and by the Chinese cardinal Thomas Tien Kenshin, though illness prevented the latter from active participation and a car accident

---

[76]Ibid., ii, pp. 42 and 44; Pulikkan, 'Indian bishops', op. cit., p. 103 note 54; Lazzarotto, 'I Vescovi Cinesi', op. cit., p. 72. The numbers given in the three works vary somewhat.

[77]Pulikkan, 'Indian bishops', op. cit., p. 103 note 54.

[78]Ibid., p. 98 note 38 and p.103 note 54.

[79]Alberigo, *Vaticano II*, iv, p. 32.

necessitated his resignation in 1963.[80] Philip Nabaa, the Melkite bishop of Beirut in Lebanon, an Arab, was one of the council's five under-secretaries, working under the Secretary-general, the Italian archbishop Pericles Felici. The Secretariat for Extraordinary Affairs, which pope John established as a mediating body between the Presidents and the Secretary-general, comprised seven cardinals none of whom was Asian.[81] The second session of the council in the autumn of 1963 saw a radical change in the council's government with the introduction of four Moderators. They formed an executive committee, responsible for determining the programme of the council's business and individually presiding over the debates, thus replacing for most purposes the rather cumbersome Council of Presidents. The same four individuals held the office of Moderator throughout the rest of the council: Cardinals Döpfner, Suenens and Lercaro from Europe and cardinal Agagianian from Armenia, sometimes described as the three Synoptics and St John! The three 'Synoptics' undoubtedly formed the driving force of the team but Agagianian also played his part.

As the first session of the council unfolded, the most distinctive figure from Asia was the Melkite patriarch of Antioch, Maximos IV, then aged 84. He led the opposition to cardinals being given precedence over patriarchs in the seating in St Peter's church, where the formal debates were held, in the order of speaking in the debates, in liturgical functions and on other occasions. He thus led the way in a certain decentralisation of the Church, a recognition that the eastern-rite Catholic churches, and by extension other churches, are churches in their own right, not just extensions of the Roman

---

[80] Alberigo, *Vatican II*, ii, pp. 56-7; Lazzarotto, 'I Vescovi Cinesi', op. cit., p. 72.

[81] Alberigo, *Vatican II*, ii, pp. 48 and 58.

church. All seven eastern-rite Catholic churches, most of whose representatives at the council were Asians, were in agreement regarding the distinctiveness of their churches and that they should form bridges to eventual reunion with the Orthodox and other eastern churches. In other respects, however, they appear divided. The representatives of the Chaldean and Armenian churches, along with some Maronites and the Ukrainians, were closer allies of Rome. The Melkites, led by Maximos IV and bishop Edelby of Edessa, and some Maronites, were the most insistent upon the autonomy of their churches. Edelby, indeed, attacked the role of 'experts living in Rome', who, he said, should keep to their place and not substitute themselves for bishops, whose view they did not represent. Maximos and Edelby, moreover, had close contacts with western bishops who were open to ecumenism. They and the other Melkite bishops resided at Salvator Mundi together with groups of various nationalities, including a dozen North American bishops, and Edelby recorded in his journal the friendliness and exchange of views among them.[82]

Patriarch Maximos and the other Melkite bishops led the attack in the council's first session on the decree on the Oriental churches, *De unitate*, which had been drawn up by the relevant preparatory commission before the council. Their criticism focused on the decree's alleged premise that in eventual reunion with the Orthodox churches, the eastern-rite Catholic churches -- sometimes called uniate churches -- were something of an embarrassment and might have to be sacrificed or would disappear. They argued, once again, that they were churches in their own right, sister churches of Rome not disposable daughters. This aggressive line, however, irritated the other eastern Catholic churches and finally the Melkites were defeated

---

[82] Ibid., ii, pp. 36, 172, 176-7, 191, 326-7, 461 and 464.

and isolated in the council debate. Ultimately, indeed, partly as a result of the Melkite attack, relations with the Orthodox church were removed from the decree, thus castrating it, and were transferred to the decree on ecumenism.[83]

In most other respects the Asian representatives in the early stages of the council appear to have acted as individuals rather than as members of national or ethnic groups. There are various reasons for this. The relative newness and minority status of Catholicism in most countries of Asia meant a certain lack of tradition and confidence. Many bishops were missionaries from Europe, often members of religious orders, and as a result had ties outside Asia. Finally, the Asian churches lacked national colleges in Rome -- apart from those of some eastern-rite Catholic churches and the newly founded Collegio Filippino -- where the bishops of a country could live together in their own environment and as a result could coalesce as a group, as happened with USA bishops at the North American College and European bishops in their national colleges.[84]

A number of the representatives of Asia, mostly missionaries of European origin, made important contributions to groups that were not limited to the Asian continent. The Dutch Capuchin Tarcisius van Valenberg, who had been Apostolic Vicar in Borneo for many years, was the founder and leader of the association of missionary bishops called 'Vriedenclub'. A loose structure, a study group more than anything else, without any formal organisation, it met regularly during the council and was very influential within progressive circles in the council. Van Valenburg was also a member of the 'Church of the Poor' group within the council and a friend of its

---

[83]Ibid., ii, pp. 317-27 and 460-8.

[84]Ibid., ii, pp. 176-7 and 191; Pulikkan, 'Indian bishops', op. cit., p. 104.

leader, Father Gauthier. Jan Schütte, Superior General of the Society of the Divine Word (SVD), who became the chief architect of the council's decree on the Missions, *Ad Gentes*, was another European missionary who had worked in Asia. He had been Apostolic Pro-Prefect of Sinsiang in China until his expulsion from the country. Of a different leaning, several bishops from the Philippines were members of the conservative group 'Coetus Patrum'.[85]

Asia also made some contribution through the 'observers' sent by various churches. Those represented in this way were the Armenian church of Lebanon and the Syriac church, and various other Orthodox and Oriental Orthodox (Monophysite) churches which, though not principally Asian churches, had members in various countries of the continent, mainly in the near East. Most Protestant churches that sent 'observers' also had congregations in Asia. Prominent among the observers was Karekin Sarkissian of the Armenian church of Lebanon. When the 'observers' were received in audience by pope John XXIII on 13 October, Sarkissian was chosen to reply to the pope on their behalf, though in the end he was not permitted to do so for reasons of protocol. Paul Verghese from India, Assistant General Secretary of WCC, represented the Syrian Jacobite Church.[86]

The Progressive Majority

The most important development at Vatican II was the emergence of the progressive majority, which rejected the decrees that had been prepared by the Curia-dominated commissions before the council and supported the more open

---

[85] Alberigo, *Vatican II*, ii, pp. 199 and 219-21.

[86] Ibid., ii, pp. 180-2; Pulikkan, 'Indian bishops', op. cit., p. 103 note 54.

and progressive ones that eventually emerged. The most prominent members of this majority, especially in the first two years of the council, were predominantly Europeans. Patriarch Maximos IV of Antioch was one of the relatively few exceptions from other continents. Nevertheless the 250 or so bishops and others representing Asia, along with those representing the other continents outside Europe, were crucial for the development of the progressive party into the majority party. There was both a similarity and a difference with Vatican I. At both councils the representatives of Asia aligned largely with the majority, but whereas at Vatican I it was with what might be called the Rome-dominated majority, at Vatican II it was with the majority led by northern Europe.

Third Session, Autumn 1964

The contribution of Asia within the progressive majority is well illustrated by the debates of the third session of the council in the autumn of 1964. We may look at this role through the debates on five decrees, which I have recently had the privilege of studying,[87] namely: *Gaudium et Spes* or 'The Church in the Modern World', Missions, The Life and Ministry of Priests, Priestly Formation, Marriage.

The Church in the Modern World

The debate on *Gaudium et Spes*, 'The Church in the Modern World', dominated the third session of the council. The debate on the other and more theological decree on the Church, *Lumen gentium*, took place for the most part earlier, in the first

---

[87]Chapter 5, 'La chiesa nelle società: *ecclesia ad extra*', Alberigo, *Vaticano II*, iv. References are given in the footnotes to the full speeches as published in: *Acta Synodalia Sacrosancti Concilii Oecumenici Vaticani II* (Vatican City, 1970-80). The chapter is forthcoming in English: Alberigo, *Vatican II*, vol. 4.

and second sessions. While *Lumen Gentium* is usually regarded as the centrepiece of the council, *Gaudium et spes* may be seen as its crown. Of all the council's sixteen decrees it accorded most closely with pope John's vision of a pastoral council. It was the first decree ever of an ecumenical council to be addressed directly not only to all Christians but also to the wider world: 'The second Vatican council now addresses itself not just to the Church's own sons and daughters and all who call on the name of Christ but to people everywhere'.[88] An unusually large number of bishops, from most parts of the world, spoke in the debate. The topics, moreover seems to have stimulated interest to an exceptional degree. This is not surprising since the large majority of the members of the council were diocesan bishops or ordinaries who would be especially interested in the work and mission of the Church in the world. The debate, too, coming in the middle of the third session of the council, was at a time of maturity for the council. The sense is of many individuals speaking with confidence and quite freely about issues that concerned them deeply, indeed passionately. The discussions are a microcosm both of the council and of the Church of the time.[89]

The views expressed by the bishops and other speakers from Asia represented a fair spectrum of the debate as a whole. In the first stage of the debate, from 20 to 23 October, when the decree as a whole was discussed, four of the forty-four speakers were from Asia. Yu Pin, the exiled archbishop of Nanking in China, regretted the absence of any explicit condemnation of Communism in the document. Speaking in the name of more than seventy bishops and others mostly from China and other parts of Asia, he urged the addition of a whole chapter on

---

[88]*Gaudium et spes*, no. 2 (*Decrees*, ii, p. 1069).
[89]Alberigo, *Vaticano II*, iv, pp. 353-4.

atheistic Communism, which he described as the culmination of all heresies, so that, among other considerations, it might satisfy all those people who 'groan under the yoke of Communism and unjustly endure unspeakable sufferings.' The recommendation was not accepted by the council. Paul Meouchi, the Maronite patriarch of Antioch, thought the decree subordinated the Church's supernatural ends too much to earthly goals:

> 'The mission of the Church is described exclusively in terms of solving the temporal problems of this world, as if the Church existed only to do works of charity or to resolve social and economic problems among people. The divine purpose, in establishing the Church, is not adequately propounded.'

He also thought the approach was too individualistic: 'The sense of the ecclesial community or the people of God in evolution is not asserted sufficiently: the schema labours under individualism.' Alphonse Mathias, bishop of the newly created diocese of Chikmagalur in Karnataka, south India, wanted more emphasis upon divine providence, especially if the decree was to have an appeal in missionary lands, where providence was accepted by almost everyone even if it should not be seen as a remedy for all evils. He also wanted more reference to papal encyclicals especially regarding their exposition of natural law. Darmojuwono, archbishop of the newly created diocese of Semarang in Indonesia, later Cardinal, criticised the decree's lack of clarity regarding the two key words of 'church' and 'world'. He also urged a better biblical basis for the decree and, regarding the way forward, he emphasised the role of the laity in an almost revolutionary way, saying that it was they who should have the main role in discerning and resolving the outstanding questions.[90]

During the next stage of the debate, when the chapters and sections of the decree were discussed individually, representatives from Asia again made a significant contribution, for the most part in what might be called the 'progressive' direction. Stanislaus Lokuang, bishop of Tainan in Taiwan (Formosa), urged the importance of thoughtful inculturation. Speaking of the cultural activity of the Church in the missions, he emphasised that every people has its own culture and the Church must respect all of them. This cultural activity, he said, is required 'for the preparation or pre-evangelization of the gentiles to hear the preaching of the gospel' and he stressed the importance of the intellectual apostolate, especially catholic universities and publications.[91]

Four bishops with sees in India spoke. Louis La Ravoire Morrow, the Salesian bishop of Krishnagar in West Bengal, originally from Texas in USA, proposed that the dialogue with the world, on which the decree spoke at length, would be possible only if we promote within Christianity 'a spirit of love rather than fear of punishments' and he urged a softening of the Church's approach to mortal sin. Dominic Athaide, the Capuchin bishop of Agra, wanted the Church to speak out more strongly against the evils of discrimination by race and colour. He was also one of the very few to praise the work of non-Christians. Thus he praised his fellow-countrymen Mahatma Gandhi and Vinobba Bhave as crusaders for social justice and better conditions of life, alongside John Kennedy and Martin Luther King and 'countless other Christians'. Duraisamy

---

[90]Ibid., iv, pp. 307, 309-13 and 315-17.

[91]Ibid., iv, pp. 339 and 341.

Lourdusamy, auxiliary bishop of Bangalore, later archbishop of Bangalore and cardinal, speaking, he said, in the name of almost all the Indian bishops present, more than sixty of them, spoke of aid between nations. Material aid to people in need, he said, is not enough. More important is:

> 'emotional integration, a sense of unity and equality among all people, whether rich or poor, prosperous or in need, healthy or sick, highest or lowest in society; that is to say, psychological help is required more than physical and material, help that comes from the heart and goes to the heart.'

Gregorios Varghese Thangalathil, better known as Benedict Mar Gregorios, the Syro-Malankara bishop of Trivandrum in Kerala, the fourth representative of India to speak, also dwelt on material conditions but was more concrete in his application. The divide between rich and poor nations, he said, is a moral issue inasmuch as the use of material things is necessary for the practice of virtues, as Thomas Aquinas stated. Without this use, moreover, an honest life becomes extremely difficult and people live in a proximate occasion of sin and spiritual harm. The tragedy, he said, is that the divide between nations exists and yet is unnecessary since the world today possesses the means for all to live decently.[92]

For Indonesia, Rudolph Staverman, vicar apostolic of Sukarnapura (today, Djajapura), who was a Franciscan missionary from the Netherlands, took quite a radical line on marriage, which was a hot topic in the debate on account of the possible revision of the Church's teaching on birth control. Speaking in the name of nine Indonesian and other bishops, he

---

[92] Ibid., iv, 323, 327, 329-31 and 345-7.

argued that marriage evolves like every historical reality and therefore the Church cannot be content with repeating earlier formulae, for if it does the teaching 'loses its pastoral effectiveness'. He wanted the commission responsible for revising the decree to take on more 'lay experts' as collaborators and not just as consultors since these lay people 'represent married people better than bishops and priests can' and they have a better knowledge of 'both the evolution of our understanding of marriage, conjugal love, fruitfulness, etc., and of the evolution of marriage as an historical reality.' Bishop Nguyen-Khac-Ngu, bishop of Long-Xuyen in Vietnam, wanted the decree, in its treatment of human solidarity, to give more attention to Asia, especially the Far East, to pay more respect to its 'personality' and spiritual values.[93]

Bishops from Asia belonging to the Oriental Catholic Churches also made a significant contribution to the debate. Ignatius Ziadé, Maronite bishop of Beirut in Lebanon, wanted a more biblical and theological exposition of the 'signs of the times' in the decree. After all, he said, the phrase 'signs of the times' comes from the gospels and the signs are not just 'created things that manifest the Creator, they are 'signs of the coming of the Lord'. He urged, too, that the main themes of the council should converge more clearly in the decree, especially the liturgy as 'the leaven of the transfiguration of history', the Church as the 'communion of the holy Trinity communicated to all people', and the eschatological sense of tradition as the 'prophecy of the economy of the Spirit'. George Hakim, Melkite bishop of Akka in Israel, criticised the decree for its lack of clarity and air of 'paternal exhortation'.[94]

---

[93] Ibid., iv, pp. 333, 336-7 and 351.
[94] Ibid., iv, pp. 320, 322 and 350-1.

Maximus IV, Melkite patriarch of Antioch in Syria, was again the most outspoken. He argued that the dialogue with the world, which the decree recommended, would be possible only if we look first to ourselves: only if, that is, we ourselves are formed and treated according to the fundamental moral principle of Christ, that he calls us friends not servants. So the 'legalist spirit', which has reigned since the sixteenth century and 'blocks the energy of both priests and laity' should be consigned to the past and in its place should reign the 'law of grace and love'. On the delicate issue of birth control he stated outright that it was causing 'a grave crisis in the christian conscience', a 'division between the official teaching of the Church and the contrary practice of the large majority of Christian families'. The increase in population in some regions condemned hundreds of millions of people to an unworthy and hopeless misery. Is this 'depressing and unnatural impasse' really the will of God? 'Frankly', he said, 'should not the official positions of the Church in this matter be revised in the light of our knowledge today, theological, medical, psychological and sociological?' On nuclear weapons he was equally forthright.

Nuclear weapons, he said, threaten to destroy humanity and if the two thousand bishops at the council from all parts of the world called for peace, they might 'change the course of history and save humanity'. Nuclear weapons will lead to a cataclysm for the world on a new scale, so that the former concept of a just war is no longer applicable. The decree, he acknowledged, speaks out against them but an even stronger and clearer 'condemnation of all nuclear, chemical and bacteriological warfare' was needed.[95]

---

[95] Ibid., iv, pp. 323, 327, 333, 336 and 348-9.

Missions

In the debate on the decree on Missions, which occupied the council from 6 to 9 November, the Taiwanese bishop Lokuang, mentioned above, played an especially important role. He had become vice-president of the conciliar commission on Missions, which had been responsible for drafting the decree up to this point, and in this capacity he and cardinal Agagianian, president of the commission, were responsible for introducing the decree to the assembly on the opening day of the debate. Agagianian, who was also Prefect of the Roman curia's Congregation for the Propagation of the Faith as well as one of the four Moderators of the council, as mentioned earlier, put his weight behind the decree, which had, earlier in the day, in an unprecedented move, been praised by the pope himself. Paul VI had come in person to the assembly, the only working session of the council (as distinct from solemn sessions to open or prorogue or conclude the council) that either he or John XXIII attended, and delivered a short speech of support for the decree. He then departed before the speeches of Agagianian and Lokuang. The latter, therefore, had the difficult task of facing, on the one hand, the expressed support of the pope and Agagianian for the decree and, on the other, the known opposition of most of the council to it. Opposition arose primarily because in the preceding summer the decree, along with several others that were regarded as of secondary importance, had been reduced to the status of a 'Set of Propositions', a brief decree that simply listed a number of points without any rounded development of them. This was the result of the so-called 'Döpfner Plan', the initiative of Cardinal Döpfner of Munich, one of the council's four Moderators, which enjoyed the support of Paul VI and whose aim was to enable the council to conclude at the end of that year 1964. The plan met with widespread resistance from the members of the council on the grounds that important topics were not being treated with sufficient seriousness and the decree on Missions was one of those about which this was particularly felt.[96]

Bishop Lokuang skillfully managed to show his sympathy with this opposition without openly rebuffing either cardinal Agagianian or Paul VI, both in his opening address and in the speech with which he wound up the debate. As a result the decree went forward to further and successful revision before the council met for the last time in 1965. Lokuang was elected to the editorial team responsible for the revision and Jan Schütte, formerly Apostolic Pro-Prefect of Sinsiang in China and at the time Superior General of the Society of the Divine Word (SVD), was elected its president. Schütte, indeed, became the key figure in the revision, providing also pleasant surroundings for meetings of the group at the Divine Word college besides lake Nemi near Rome.[97]

In the short debate on the decree, twenty-eight speeches were made in addition to the opening and closing addresses of Agagianian and Lokuang. Seven of the twenty-eight speakers represented Asian sees: a high proportion, once again. Namely, the same bishop Lokuang, who spoke in the middle of the debate in a private capacity; Bishop Picachy of Jamshedpur, later cardinal archbishop of Calcutta in India; Cardinal Doi of Tokyo, Japan; and four European missionary bishops, Pietro Massa and John Baptist Velasco of the dioceses of Nanyang and Hsiamen in China, both of whom had been expelled from the country; Nicholas Geise, bishop of Bogor in Indonesia, and Peter

---

[96] Alberigo, *Vatican II*, iii, pp. 390-3 and 415-16; Alberigo, *Vaticano II*, iv, pp. 358-64.

[97] Alberigo, *Vaticano II*, iv, pp. 365, 371-2 and 605-16.

Carretto, vicar-apostolic of Rajaburi in Thailand. Most of them supported the majority of the council in their disappointment with the short decree. Geise was the most severe, quoting Virgil, 'The mountains give birth and there comes forth a ridiculous mouse!' In other respects there was both agreement and differences of emphasis. Massa and Picachy wanted the decree to say more about the role of catechists. Carretto, speaking in the name of the bishops of Thailand, Laos and Cambodia, regretted the failure to mention the 'twinning' of parishes and dioceses, which provided mission lands with much material, psychological and personal help from traditionally Catholic countries. He praised, too, the work of various European and North American foundations that provided help – spiritual, material and in personnel – for the missions. Picachy, however, reminded the fathers that missions give as well as receive: they are 'a privilege not a burden for the Church; they contribute much to its vitality, fervour and catholicity'. Velasco thought the decree should say something about nationalism, which has 'an intimate connection with the work of evangelization', and the rights of migrants to be treated as full citizens. Cardinal Doi emphasised the importance of knowing and embracing the local culture. Massa and Lokuang, on the other hand, warned against ill-conceived adaptation. Massa wanted the decree to state more clearly that there can be no compromise on the 'essential elements of the Christian religion', otherwise a diluted version of Christianity arises, indeed there should rather be adaptation in all things to the Gospel. Lokuang, in a similar vein, said that while converts to Christianity are not obliged to renounce their own culture as such, nevertheless they are bound to renounce 'everything in the culture that is erroneous and inauthentic and irreconcilable with the new life in Christ'.[98]

Priests

In the short debates on the two decrees 'The Life and Ministry of Priests' and 'Priestly Formation', which took place on various days in October and November, Asian sees were represented by 2 of the 41 speakers in the first debate – Joseph Evangelisti of Meerut in India and Francis Ayoub, the Maronite bishop of Aleppo in Syria -- and 2 out of 32 in the second: Joseph Gopu of Hyderabad in India and Paul Sani of Denpasar in Bali, Indonesia. All of them were indigenous Asians except the bishop of Meerut who was Italian by birth. Their comments are notable for their foresight of developments in the Church after the council.

Speaking about the work of priests, Evangelisti wanted the missionary nature of the priesthood to be stressed and he was one of the few speakers to mention priests' responsibilities outside the Catholic fold. Priests, he said, are co-workers with their bishop in caring for the good of the whole world, not just for that of the diocese, since 'the whole human world was created to form the new people of God'. Gopu wanted more inculturation for seminaries. These, he said, 'in the missions should not try to imitate European seminaries exactly or slavishly' and he recommended pastoral work for the seminarians during the vacations, 'catechizing boys and catechumens, teaching liturgical singing, instructing altar servers, and so on.' Sani spoke in a similar vein. He suggested that seminarians live at home and help their parish priests during the vacations and that there should be a year's pastoral or

---

[98] Ibid., iv, pp. 366-8 and 370.

practical work after the seminary and ordination to the priesthood. He also recommended that seminarians do all their studies before ordination in their own country and go abroad for further studies only afterwards.[99]

Marriage

By the third session of the council the decree on marriage had the status of a *votum*, a guide giving principles for the forthcoming revision of Canon Law, and was no longer intended to be a full conciliar decree. Marriage had already been treated in *Gaudium et Spes*. In the short debate on the document towards the end of the session, Asia was represented by two of the 14 speakers: Paul Taguchi, archbishop of Osaka in Japan, and Adrian Djajasepoetra, archbishop of Djakarta in Indonesia.

Taguchi, who was a member of the conciliar commission responsible for the *Votum*, and who spoke in the debate in the name of 'many bishops of Japan and other countries', was positively encouraging of mixed marriages at least in missions lands. They often lead to conversions to the Catholic faith, he said, and the liturgy of the solemn nuptial Mass is attractive to non-Christians and moves them towards the Catholic religion, thereby greatly helping the propagation of the faith. He also urged more efficiency in dealing with marriage cases in church courts. Djajasepoetra, speaking in the name of twenty-nine bishops from Indonesia and elsewhere in Asia, was trenchant regarding the need to adapt teaching about marriage to the local situation. He thought the definition of marriage at the beginning of the *votum*, as 'a holy contract of love, instituted by God for the worthy propagation of the human race and the protection of the sacred law of life', was too western and inapplicable to

---

[99]Ibid., iv, pp. 375-7, 379-80, 386-7, 389 and 391-2.

places such as Indonesia, Africa, Pakistan, India and China – inapplicable, therefore to most of the world! He quoted the words of a Pakistani woman to westerners, 'You contract marriage because you love, we love because we are joined in marriage'. As a better definition for marriage he suggested, 'A sacred and human community of life between man and woman, instituted by God for the establishment of a family.' It is unrealistic and unfair to give primacy to love, he argued, since outside the West marriage is often settled by the couple's parents: mutual love grows gradually as the fruit of marriage.[100]

Conclusion

These five debates in the third year of the council – on *Gaudium et Spes*, Missions, The Life and Ministry of Priests, Priestly Formation, and Marriage – form but a small part of the monumental event of Vatican II. In addition to the speeches actually made in the debates, many individuals wanted to speak and submitted texts of their intended addresses but shortage of time and the resulting closure of debates prevented their delivery. A much larger number of individuals or groups submitted written comments, which, like all the speeches, whether delivered or not, should have been taken into consideration by the conciliar commissions responsible for revising the decrees. All of these contributions can be found in the printed *Acta* of the council, largely thanks to the prodigious editorial work of Monsignor Carbone.[101] There was, too, the council that went on outside the *aula*, the formal debating chamber set up in the nave of St Peter's church: in the bars set up in the side-chapels of St Peter's, where many participants met after or even during the debates in the *aula*, in the meetings of

---

[100] Ibid., iv, pp. 407 and 409-10.

[101] *Acta Synodalia*, as in p. 70 note 87 above.

national episcopal conferences, in informal discussions among friends, through the mass media, and so on. What has been suggested above, therefore, is very much only the tip of an iceberg, or rather one peak in a mountain range. What, too, was the influence of the speeches that we have looked at briefly? How far did the members of the council, especially the members of the conciliar commissions, pay attention to them?[102] The speeches are more of a window into the council than a precise measure of influence. Then there is the question of the reception of Vatican II after the council had ended. Reception is an integral part any council, especially an ecumenical council. What has been the role of Asia in the reception of Vatican II? These are large and important questions to which answers have not been attempted here but which will surely continue to be the subject of research for years to come.[103]

Despite these obvious limitations, it may be hoped that this lecture has shown, from a few pieces of the great patchwork quilt of Vatican II, that Asia made an important and distinctive contribution, that the council saw a major righting in the balance of the Church, in the direction of what was to be found in microcosm in the councils of the early Church: a righting and balancing that has continued in the years since the council and looks set to continue into the new millennium.

---

[102] For the continuing Asian contribution into the fourth and last session of the council in the autumn of 1965, see Alberigo, *Vaticano II*, vol. 5, passim.

[103] For some of the work already done, see p. 62 note 68 above. Two further publications regrettably came to my attention too late for consideration: P. Pulikkan, *Indian Church at Vatican II: A Historical-Theological Study of the Indian Participation in the Second Vatican Council*, (Trichur: Marynooth Publications, 2001); P.C. Phan, 'Reception of Vatican II in Asia: Historical and Theological Analysis', *Gregorianum*, 83 (2002), pp. 269-85.

Conclusion and the Future

The three chapters tell their own story. There is hardly the need of a Conclusion.

In the councils of the early Church, Asia made the largest contribution of all the continents in terms of participants and of theological input. The influence of the eastern church was predominant. The centre of the Church is more accurately seen as located in Asia Minor rather than – following common Eurocentric approaches to geography and history – around the Mediterranean sea. The eastern face of Greek thought also pushes the centre into Asia. Just how far East is illustrated by the spread of Christianity into India and the far East, most notably the expansion of the Syriac (Nestorian) church into China, and by Manichaeism, which must be seen within the context of Christianity and which, originating in Mesopotamia, spread both East and west, so linking western Asia, where the Church was most established, with eastern. Finally, the decrees issued by these early councils reveal not only the theological content of the eastern and Asian church but also an eastern mentality, perhaps best seen in a mainly cyclical view of life, in spaciousness and flexibility of language, and in the quest for accommodation and unanimity.

Following the sad schism between the churches of East and West beginning in the eleventh century, and the Islamic conquests of much of the Byzantine world, the centre of Christianity moved to West Europe. The major councils, best described as general councils of the western church, were held in Rome, France, Germany and Switzerland. Almost all the participants were Europeans. Nevertheless the western Church clung to its Asian roots, hesitant to outgrow them. It accorded greater status to the councils of the early Church than to its own. It sensed its own insecurity and remained in awe of its eastern and Asian past. In the sixteenth century, the council of Trent began by affirming the Nicene creed, thus placing itself in the mainstream of the early Church, and, while benefiting from many insights of the Reformation, in various ways also preserved the catholicity of the Church against an excessively Eurocentric theology and spirituality.

By the time of the first and second Vatican councils, Christianity had developed into the largest and most widespread world religion. The influence of Asia began to be felt again more directly. It provided a significant number of bishops at the first council and they made a modest contribution to the proceedings. At the second Vatican council the number of participants from Asia – especially indigenous Asians as distinct from European missionaries – grew significantly, as did their contributions, especially as the council progressed. The council contributed to rebalancing the Church away from Europe, towards Asia and the other continents.

What of the future? Maybe the next council will take place in Manila or Delhi, returning the Church to the Asian location of its first ecumenical council in Nicaea. The churches of Asia have already played a prominent role in the reception of Vatican II and this will surely grow, much to the benefit of the wider church. The second Vatican council, as well as the caution of the councils held after the beginning of the East-West schism, especially those of the Middle Ages, encourage a certain liberation from what is sometimes called western colonial theology and spirituality. Nevertheless, in view of Asia's unique and profoundly beneficial contribution to Christianity through the early councils, this liberation will be healthier for all if it includes prominently a recovery of Asian roots as well as any necessary rejection of what is onesidedly western.

The Church certainly cannot be called too Asian—to answer the question provocatively posed in the book's title. On the other hand, the councils show that Asia has been well represented in this key dimension of the Church's history.

Index

Agagianian, Cardinal, 65, 66, 76, 77
Agatho, Pope, 30
Aleppo, 18
Alexander the Great, 18, 22
Alexandria, 22, 23, 25
Ambrosiaster, 24
Ancyra (Ankara), Council (314), 20
Anglican-Roman Catholic International Commission (ARCIC), 37
Antioch, 22, 25, 26, 27
  Council (268), 19
Aristotle, 17, 46
Arius, 19, 22
Armenia, 28, 66
Armenian church, 41, 42, 53, 69
Asia, *passim,* Definition of, 14, 23
Asia Minor, 14, 20, 28, 85
Athaide, Dominic, 73
Augustine of Hippo, 29, 41, 53
Averröes, 46
Avicenna, 46
Ayoub, Francis, 80

Babylon, 24
Barnabò, Cardinal, 59
Baronius, Cesare, 35

Basel-Florence (1431-45), Council, 33, 36, 41
Bazin, Victor, 62
Bellarmine, Robert, 35
Bhave, Vinobba, 73
Borneo, 68
Buddhism, 25, 62

Cambodia, 79
Carretto, Peter, 79
Cathars, 39
Celestine I, Pope, 29
Chalcedon (451), Council, 13 to 16, 25 to 30, 38, 48
Chaldaean church, 41, 58, 67
Charlemagne, 21
China, 23-24, 58, 62, 65, 68, 78, 82, 85
Christology, 19-32, 41, 51-52, 63. See also, *Filioque*
Congar, Yves, 36
Constance (1414-18), Council, 33-34, 41, 48, 54
Constantine I, Emperor, 16
Constantine IV, Emperor, 16
Constantine of Nakoleia, 28
Constantinople, 15, 16, 21, 22, 25, 45, 56
Constantinople I (381), Council, 13 to 16, 21, 22, 26, 29, 39, 48, 51, 57
Constantinople II (553),

Council, 13 to 16, 23, 27, 30, 48
Constantinople III (680-1) Council, 13 to 16, 25, 27, 28, 30, 48
Constantinople IV (869-70), Council, 13, 33, 34, 36, 48
Constantinople (1341), Council, 37
Constantinople (1351), Council, 37
Coptic church, 27, 41, 42
Crusades, 40, 41, 43, 46 to 49, 73
Cyril of Alexandria, 25, 29

Damascus, 28
Daniélou, Jean, 62
Darmojuwono, Archbishop, 72
Delhi, 63, 86
De Lubac, Henri, 62
Djajasepoetra, Adrian, 81, 82
Doi, Cardinal, 62, 78
Döpfner, Julius, 66, 77

Ecumenical Council, Definition of, 15, 26, 27, 33, 38, 44, 48, 50, 51, 83, 84
Edelby, Bishop, 67
Eleusius, Bishop, 21
Ephesus (431), Council, 13, 14, 16, 22 to 27, 29, 30, 38, 41, 48

Ephesus II (449), 'Robber' Council, 27
Eugenius IV, Pope, 41
Eusebius of Caesarea, 19, 24
Evangelisti, Joseph, 80

Felici, Pericles, 66
Filioque, 21, 51
Flavian, patriarch of Constantinople, 30
Florence (1439-45) Council, 33, 36, 41, 42, 43, 53
Formosa, 61, 62. See Taiwan
Frederick II, Emperor, 40

Galerius, Emperor, 16
Gandhi, Mahatma, 73
Gauthier, Paul, 69
Geise, Nicholas, 78
Gopu, Joseph, 80
Gracias, Cardinal, 62
Greece, 14, 17, 18, 46
Gregory VII Pope, 53
Greek Language, 18, 19, 23, 31, 32, 85
Greek Philosophy/ thought, 11, 17, 18, 31, 85
Guardini, Romano, 62

Hadrian I Pope, 30
Hakim, George, 75
Hecataeus, 14, 23
Hieria (754), Council, 28
Hinduism, 25
Homoousios, 19, 20, 29, 32

Hong Kong, 61
Hus, John, 41

Ibas of Edessa, 23, 27
India, 11, 25, 58, 59, 62, 63, 65, 69, 72, 73, 78, 80, 82, 85
Indo-China, 58
Indonesia, 23, 58, 72, 74, 78, 80, 82, 85. See also, Borneo
Indus valley, 18
Innocent IV, Pope, 40
Inquisition, 47, 49
Irene, Empress, 16, 28, 30
Islam, 29, 37, 45, 46, 85

Japan, 61, 78, 81
Jassy (1642), Council, 37
Jerusalem, 19, 28
Jerusalem (1672), Council, 37
Jews, 29, 42, 46, 49
John Paul ii, Pope, 48
John XXIII, Pope, 60, 64, 65, 69, 71, 77
John Damascene, 28
Justinian I, Emperor, 16, 27, 30

Kennedy, John, 73
King, Martin Luther, 73
Knights Templar, 41
Korea, 58

Laos, 79
La Ravoire Morrow, Louis, 61, 73
Lateran I (1123), Council, 33, 35, 36, 39, 43, 48, 49
Lateran II (1139), Council, 33, 35, 39, 48
Lateran III (1179), Council, 33, 35, 39, 48
Lateran IV (1215), Council, 33, 35, 39, 40, 48, 49
Lateran V (1512-17), Council, 33, 35, 36, 43, 49
Lebanon, 66, 69, 75
Leo I, Pope, 30
Lercaro, Giacomo, 66
Lokuang, Stanislaus, 73, 77, 78, 79
Lourdusamy, Duraisamy, 74
Lyons I (1245), Council, 33, 35, 40, 45, 48
Lyons II (1274), Council, 33, 35-36, 40, 48, 53

Macedonians, 21
Malaysia, 23
Mani, 24
Manichaeism, 29, 85
Manila, 58, 86
Marcion, Emperor, 16
Maronite Church, 41, 61, 67, 72, 75, 80
Mary, 62. See also *Theotokos*
Massa, Pietro, 78, 79
Mathias, Alphonse, 72
Maximus the Confessor, 28
Maximus IV, patriarch of

Antioch, 61, 66, 67, 70
Melkite, church, 58, 67, 68, 76
Meouchi, Paul, 72
Mesopotamia, 24, 85
Meurin, Leo, 59
Michael VIII Palaeologus, Emperor, 40
Mongols, 45
Monophysites, 26, 27, 69
Monothelites, 27

Nabaa, Philip, 66
Neocaesarea (315/324) Council, 20
Nestorians, 23, 25, 85
Nestorius, 22, 29
Nguyen-Khac-Ngu, Michael, 75
Nicaea I (325), Council, 11, 13 to 16, 19, 20, 26, 29, 32, 34, 36, 39, 43, 48, 51, 57, 86
Nicaea II (787), Council, 13, 14, 16, 28, 29, 30, 33, 34, 36, 43, 48
Niš, 16

Oriental Orthodox churches, 34, 38, 62, 69
Oriental (Eastern-rite) Catholic Churches, 58, 61, 65 to 68, 75, 76
Orthodox Church, 34, 37, 38, 40, 41, 51, 61, 67, 68

Ossius (Hosius) of Cordoba, 19, 29

Pakistan, 82
Paul of Samosata, 19
Paul of Tarsus, 53
Paul V, Pope, 35
Paul VI, Pope, 36, 37, 77, 78
Persia, 16, 18, 23, 24, 28
Peter Lombard, 40
Philippines, 58, 61, 69
Photius, patriarch of Constantinople, 13
Picachy, Lawrence, 78, 79
Pisa (1511-12), Council, 43
Pius IX, Pope, 55
Pius XII, Pope, 42, 43, 62
Plato, 17
Pneumatomachi, 21
Podipara, Placid, 11, 65
Pomponazzi, 43
Poona, Papal Athenaeum, 62, 63
Pulcheria, Empress, 16, 30
Purkowerto, 61

Ratzinger, Joseph, 38
Roman Curia, 55, 58, 60, 62, 64, 69, 77
Roman edition, 35
Rome, 11, 22, 33, 35, 40, 46, 55, 63, 67, 68, 78, 85
Russia, 45

Sani, Paul, 80, 81

Index

Sarkissian, Karekin, 69
Schütte, Jan, 69, 78
Sophronius, patriarch of Jerusalem, 28
Staverman, Rudolph, 74
Steins, Walter, 59
Suenens, Leo, Josef, 66
Syria, 14, 19, 22, 23, 28, 76, 80
Syriac church, 23, 69, 85
Syrian Jacobite Church, 69
Syro-Malabar rite, 11
Syro-Malankara rite, 74

Taguchi, Paul, 81
Taipei, Archbishop of, 62
Taiwan, 73. See Formosa
Tappouni, Cardinal, 65
Tartars, 45
Tertullian, 19, 29
Thailand, 79
Thangalathil, Gregorios Varghese, 74
Theodore of Mopsuestia, 22, 23, 27
Theodoret of Cyrrhus, 23, 27
Theodosius I, Emperor, 16
Theodosius II, Emperor, 16
Theotokos, 22, 25
Thomas Aquinas, 41, 74
Thomas of Claudiopolis, 28
Tibet, 23
Tien Kenshin, Thomas, 65

Toledo III (589), Council, 21
Trent, (1545-63), Council, 33, 36, 42, 50, 51 to 54, 59, 86
Trullo (692), Council, 13
Turkey, 15, 19, 22, 28

Ukrainian Church, 67
Uniate churches, see Oriental Catholic Churches

Van Valenberg, Tarcisius, 68
Vatican I (1869-70), Council, 33, 36, 55 to 60, 70, 86
Vatican II (1962-5), Council, 11, 36, 55, 57, 59 to 83, 86
Velasco, John Baptist, 78
Verghese, Paul, 69
Vienne, (1311-12), Council, 33, 35, 41, 48, 49
Vietnam, 60, 75
Vigilius, Pope, 27, 30
Virgil, 79

Willebrands, Johannes, 36
World Council of Churches (WCC), 63, 69
Wyclif, John, 41

Yu Pin, Paul, 71
Yussef, Gregory, 58

Ziadé, Ignatius, 75